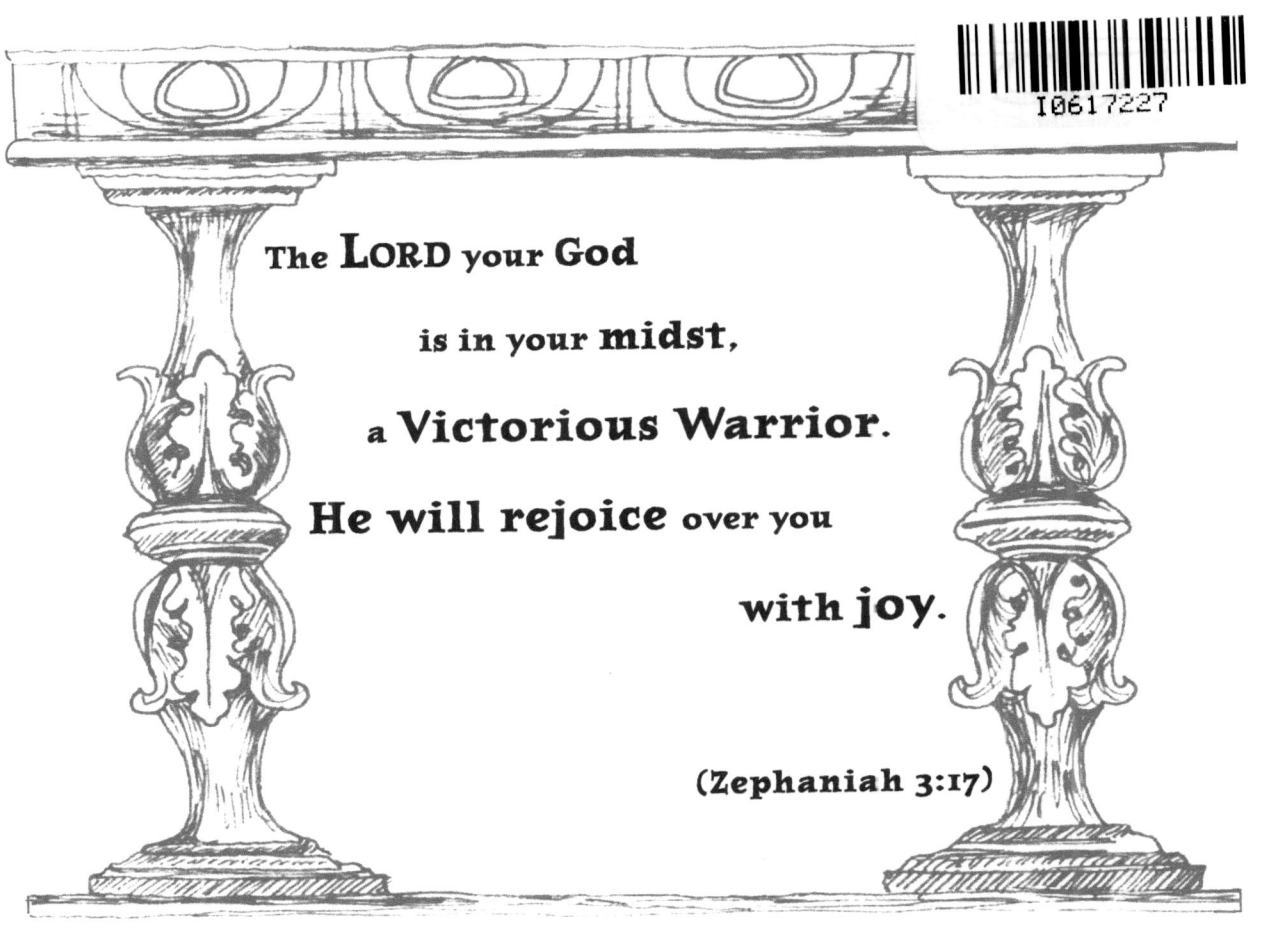

The LORD your God

is in your **midst**,

a **Victorious Warrior**.

He will rejoice over you

with **joy**.

(Zephaniah 3:17)

THE
VICTORIOUS
WARRIOR

Challenging Young People
to Aim toward the Good

Jerry and Michelle Shelfer

Sebastopol, California
2024

THE VICTORIOUS WARRIOR
Challenging Young People to Aim toward the Good
by Jerry and Michelle Shelfer

Copyright © 2024 Jerry and Michelle Shelfer
ISBN: 979-8-9897621-2-5

Published by

RAELOCH
PUBLISHING CO.

Dedication

This book is gratefully dedicated to Ivan Githinji of Kenya, Africa, at whose urging it was written. We pray that God will hear his plea for all of Africa to come to know Messiah Jesus and will bless his ministry to the youth.

We further dedicate this book to our thirteen (and counting) grandchildren. We pray that they may stand throughout their lives under the banner of the Victorious Warrior, Jesus.

CONTENTS

To Parents and Teachers

THANK YOU FOR ENTRUSTING your beloved young person to our care. This book comes from our recognition that young people today desperately need adults to tell them the truth and guide them through the crazy world into which they are coming of age. They need good, solid Biblical teaching to combat the godless and unhealthy messaging of the culture. We join our voices with yours and the voices of all who are addressing this need. Our desire is to give youth the tools to make good choices for the best outcomes in life.

This book is our answer to a direct request we received from a devoted Christian youth leader living in Kenya. His name is Ivan. Ivan read our first book about healing from the hurt of abortion. He told us he needed a book that would act as a sort of "preventive medicine" for the youth in his community—to help them get and stay on the right track in life *before* they get to the point that abortion is considered.

In this book, we offer the development of a warrior's mindset as a way to inculcate noble character into young people so that they can take their place as contributing members of society and the Body of Christ. We invite them to explore the spiritual life, and we guide them through a Biblical understanding of God, directing their attention toward the Victorious Warrior, Jesus, and the age-old battle against evil. We present readers with story examples, good and bad, directing them toward an ideal of truth, excellence, and service to others, as perfectly exemplified in the Victorious Warrior himself, Jesus. He is our exalted example, leader, help, and friend.

In using the model of the warrior, we absolutely *do not* encourage conflict with others. This book is not intended to promote war or conflict of any sort except that conflict which takes place in the spirit realm between the forces of evil and the God of the Bible, as described in Ephesians 6:12. This book is unapologetically Christian, holding to orthodox Christian theology such as is expressed in the Apostles' Creed. You can feel confident that this book will not take your youth down any theological rabbit holes.

The Victorious Warrior tackles some challenging topics in an age-appropriate way for the reader aged thirteen through eighteen. These topics include social-media use, sex, and drugs and alcohol. The purpose of broaching these topics is to instill the need for self-control as part of the warrior's mindset that values sobriety and godliness. Youths are particularly vulnerable to addiction, so we devote some attention to preventive measures in those areas. The topic of abortion is also broached. We feel that if we don't offer a Biblical view of these topics, young people will get their teachings from other sources that may not be God-honoring.

Revelation 12:11 says that we win in the Great Battle of good against evil by the blood of the Lamb and by the word of our testimony. For that reason, we have woven our own story into our teachings.

We encourage you to use *The Victorious Warrior* in groups and allow for free discussion on the topics raised. The chapters are intended to generate conversation in a group setting or with parents and family. You will find supplemental materials at our website: VictoriousWarrior.org.

We introduce a full Gospel message to our readers, and we hope that you will be a help for them or help them find suitable people to answer questions they may have about Jesus and the Bible.

We also hope that readers pull out their colored pens and pencils and engage with the illustrations, which were made for that purpose. We hope that the books end up fully colored in, scribbled on, and filled with the readers' margin notes.

As you see your youth begin to understand and practice aiming toward the good, using their code, and seeking the kingdom of God and his righteousness, be generous with your encouragement. Celebrate them when they make good decisions. Thank you again for coming alongside your young warriors as they grow with us into mighty, mature, Jesus-focused adults.

Jerry and Michelle Shelfer
Prepare a Room Ministries

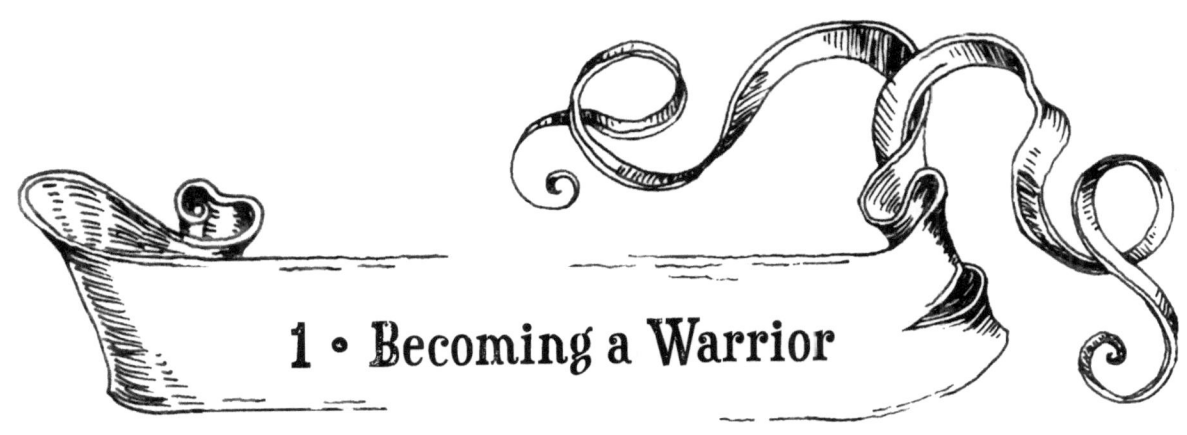

1 • Becoming a Warrior

Dear Young Person,

You are about to embark on a challenging, thought-provoking, and possibly life-changing journey. Ready? Let's begin with a thought experiment. For just a moment imagine yourself in another world: In this world, you are a valiant warrior. You are decked out in shining armor from head to toe, with a flashing blade by your side. Maybe you're mounted upon a high-spirited horse. You are on a special mission with a highly trained team, under orders from the king himself. You have been chosen for this mission because you've proven yourself well trained, loyal, and a person of the highest character. The king knows that with his help and your special training, you will complete your mission and be victorious.

You are invited to start becoming the warrior you just imagined yourself to be. Let's look at what a warrior is. Warriors have a strong sense of purpose. They train themselves to think quickly on their feet and solve problems in an ever-changing battle landscape. They develop tools to help them make the best choices for any circumstance. They learn to work well with their fellow warriors and to follow special codes of conduct.

Warriors have a higher calling. They serve as protectors, and they are aware of the needs of those around them. They use their training and excellence to be of service to others, and they are keenly aware of their role in helping to further the good in society. This is all part of what we call the *warrior's mindset*.

The word *warrior* brings all sorts of images to our minds—images of the mighty Zulu of Africa, or the Samurai of Japan, or the European medieval knights in their suits of armor. Men and women alike have been warriors. We can find warriors facing battles in all eras of history and all across the globe. One thing they have in common is that they prepare themselves physically, mentally, and morally for battle against their enemy. The best of them have developed a keen warrior's mindset, trained for victory.

Your Battles

Not every battle takes place on a battlefield during wartime. In fact, in your personal life, you face many challenges and obstacles every day—these challenges and obstacles can also be seen as battles. For example, you may be battling pressure from others to act in ways you know are wrong. You may be battling temptation to indulge habits that are not good for you. You may be battling fear of rejection. There are so many ways that your life experiences can show up as battles.

What if you were able to face these battles knowing that you are equipped with the best skills and tactics to make good choices? The warrior's mindset gives you a new way of seeing your battles so you can face them head-on. This mindset can serve you well throughout your life, whatever battles may come. It will put you on the path to your best life—a life of victory.

Games We Play

You're good at games. You've probably played many. You know what it's like to learn the rules, struggle to overcome your opponent, and use your best efforts to win—whether it's card games or video games or chess or checkers or dodgeball or capture the flag. You've learned that you need to know what the game is about, the lay of the land, how it is played, the pitfalls, and how to think ahead in order to win. You don't always win, though, so you've also

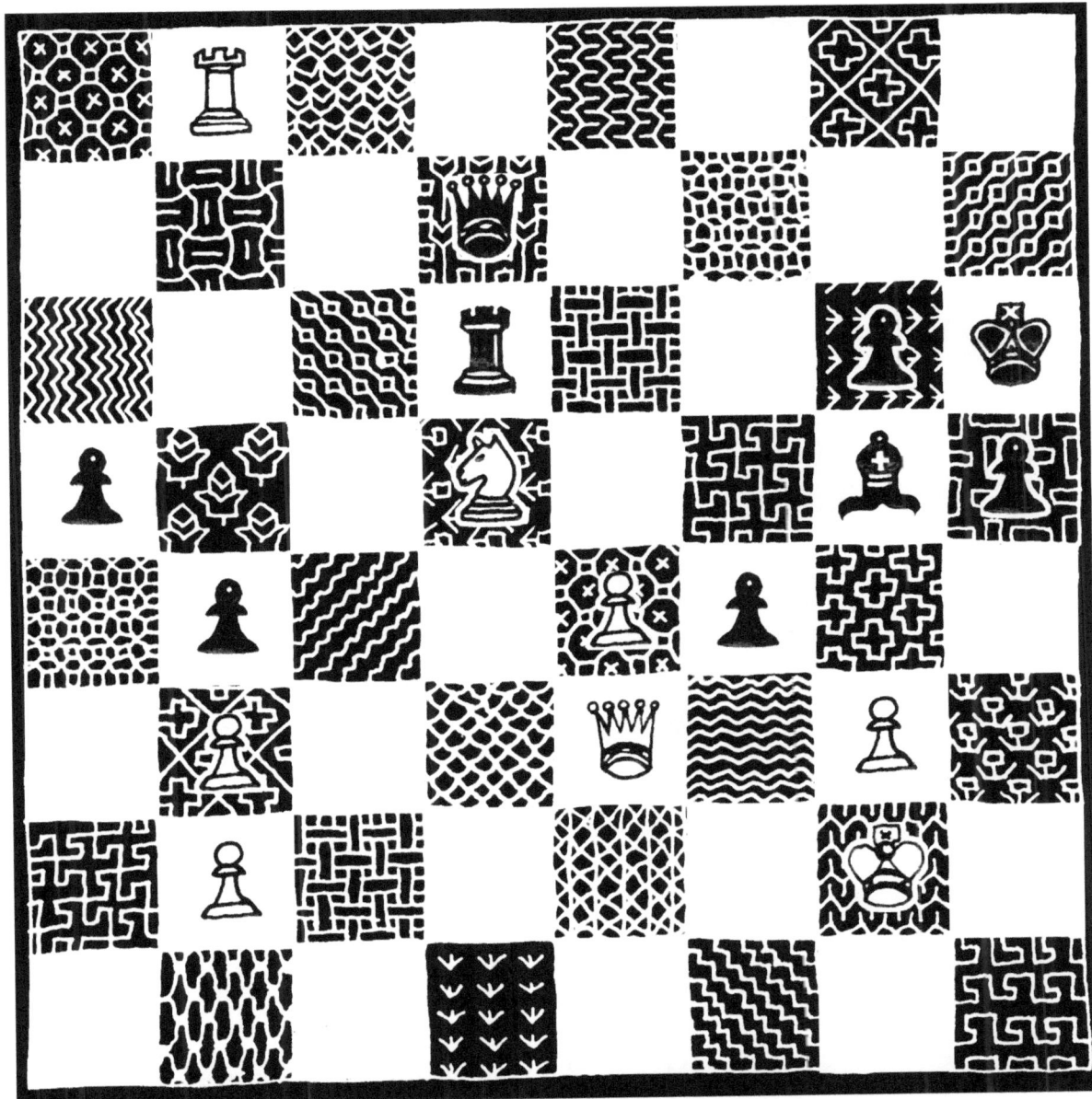

learned how to deal with losing—how to get up from your disappointments, dust yourself off, and try again.

Games can be seen as a type of battle, and playing games is a great way to learn about strategy and winning and losing. The lessons you learn while playing games can also be used in real-life situations. When you are presented with choices in life, you can stop and strategize your best move. You have goals, and sometimes obstacles get thrown in your path. You want to make the best choices to overcome those obstacles so you can achieve your goals and win.

An Invisible Battle

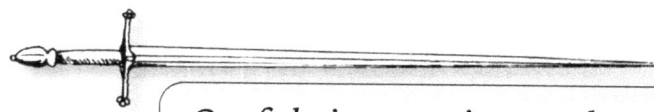

Our fight is not against people on earth.... We are fighting against the spiritual powers of evil in the heavenly places. (**Ephesians 6:12**)[1]

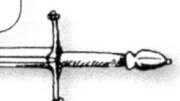

Let's talk about one particular battle—a very special battle. A battle that just happens to be the most important battle of all. And it is no game—this battle is very real. It does not take place in the physical world. It takes place in an unseen realm, and it is raging everywhere. This battle is a conflict between two powerful forces that have been going at it for a very long time.

Across a vast landscape, the warriors clash and thunder at each other with the clatter of swords against shields. Horses' hooves batter the bruised earth as they storm over this battlefield. Banners representing the two sides wave furiously over a troubled terrain. Some in this battle lie wounded, while others find their way to victory. The cries of the defeated mingle with shouts of triumph as ground is taken and lost.

The beginnings of this battle are shrouded in the mists of an ancient past, but the battle is raging even now in an unseen realm—the realm of the spiritual. The spiritual world exists right alongside the physical world we can see and touch. But even though the battle is invisible, it impacts the physical world of people's daily lives in very visible and meaningful ways.

We will call this invisible contest the Great Battle. The Great Battle is the age-old struggle between good and evil, and it is going on at this very moment. Whether or not you want to be in this battle, *you are in it.* Why say that you are in the Great Battle? Well, let's trace it back to where your life began, and we'll see just how you got here.

---

1. Words from the Bible are set apart with swords as you see here.

Your Beginnings

Everyone enters into the Great Battle the same way. Let's look at your beginnings. When you were born, you were the center of the universe. You were nothing but an adorable bundle of bodily urges in need of immediate attention, and when you cried out, the grown-ups attended to your every need. Your cries said:

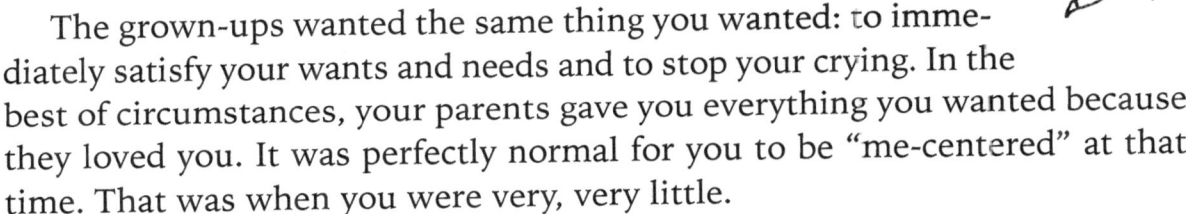

- "Feed me!"

- "Change my diaper!"

- "Pay attention to me!"

The grown-ups wanted the same thing you wanted: to immediately satisfy your wants and needs and to stop your crying. In the best of circumstances, your parents gave you everything you wanted because they loved you. It was perfectly normal for you to be "me-centered" at that time. That was when you were very, very little.

But as you got a bit older, you were encouraged to see that the world didn't revolve around you. And as time went along, more was expected of you. When you cried, the grown-ups did not respond as quickly as before. You still expected them to come running. So, maybe you screamed louder and pounded your fists, but you got less and less satisfaction. You learned to pitch a good fit and throw temper tantrums, but these behaviors were only less likely to get you what you wanted. When things didn't go your way, maybe you resorted to biting or pinching or breaking toys as a solution. You were ready to do anything to get your way.

Finally, you learned the rules of the game. You learned what was right and what was wrong—the difficult lessons that would take you from being a me-centered baby to becoming a maturing young person aware of the world around you and ready to take your place in it. Some learned this lesson easily, and others—well, not so much.

Hopefully, your parents helped you make that difficult transition. They scolded you when you hurt others and praised you when you were generous.

To continue to baby you would have handicapped your growth, so your parents pushed you out of your comfort zone and spurred you on toward maturity. They tried their best to civilize you. At least, I hope they did. If they didn't, it's not too late. You can learn now.

And so, you grew up bit by bit. The more time passed, the more choices you made. You experienced a strange new feeling that babies don't have: by doing what you *ought to* do instead of only doing what you *feel like* doing, you developed a sense of self-worth that comes from doing what you know is right. You learned the golden rule: to treat others the way you want to be treated.

The older you grew, the more you became responsible for your choices, both good and bad. Being responsible for your choices, you began to struggle between making right choices and making wrong choices. And when you struggled between right and wrong, *that was when you stepped onto the battlefield of that Great Battle.*

Where You Are Now

And here you are now, a young adult, and you've made a lot of choices along the way as you've grown up. Who are you? You are one of a kind. You have special God-given talents that are unique to you alone, with your own set of strengths to develop and weaknesses to overcome.

You have been given the opportunity in life to make many choices, and you've been given free will. What sort of choices will you make? It's up to you. How you choose will determine how that Great Battle plays out in your life. This is why it is important to think deeply about your choices. You should make your choices carefully and thoughtfully, as a warrior would in battle. If you want to live your best life, you need to step up and approach the challenge of making good choices as one training to be a warrior.

> Learning to be a warrior in the Great Battle is exactly what this book is all about.

Learning to be a warrior in the Great Battle is exactly what this book is all about. In this book, you're going to pursue the warrior's mindset. You will learn from the examples (both good and bad) of those who have gone before you. You will gather the warrior's tools needed to be effective. You will discover exactly what the battle is that you are fighting. And you will encounter Jesus, the mighty Victorious Warrior, and his kingdom—the kingdom of God. By aligning yourself with the Victorious Warrior and seeking his help, you will achieve ultimate victory and live your best life.

This book is *not* about training you to physically fight or serve in a war between armies on a physical battlefield and is *absolutely not* meant to encourage you to get into conflict with other people. But instead, it is about developing in you the tools to make good choices and grow the special inner character that true warriors possess.

So, are you ready to become a warrior?

Let's start with a story of two characters who didn't quite learn their lessons when they were young, and let's see what sort of trouble they got into. Maybe you can learn from their mistakes.

Some questions for you:

1. Discuss a battle you are facing in your everyday life.

2. Do you remember a moment when you went from being me-centered to being aware of other people's needs?

3. What life lessons have you learned from playing your favorite games?

2 • Two Who Lost Their Way

There once was a young boy who lived with his mother and father in a little cottage near the edge of the piney woods. He spent most of his days alone, daydreaming about being a mighty warrior. What set this boy apart from others his age was that his legs were rather long. His legs were so long that he was able to jump over puddles, fences, or anything else that got in his way. Life was easy for him.

When the boy got older, his parents began to worry because they wished by then he would have become more useful. There was much work to do on their land, and they tried to teach him how to do the many chores around the little cottage. But alas, when he wasn't making up adventures for himself, he was busy reading books about the lives of the knights and their quests. He lived in his dreams, where he was already a knight living a life of adventure, and to him, all the creatures of the woods seemed to agree.

When he would return home after a long day of slaying dragons, jousting on his trusty steed, and searching for buried treasure in the woods, the boy's father would sigh and ask wearily, "Where have you been all day? Did you get any work done?"

With his head full of adventure and the life of an adventurer, his real life at the little cottage was a bore for him because it was filled with responsibilities that took him away from his daydreaming.

Besides the chores he was expected to do, there were lots of rules:

- "Do your homework!"
- "Finish your peas!"
- "Get to bed early!"

The long-legged boy was not so keen on rules. He preferred the freedom of the forest, and so he spent most of his time away from home.

Years passed. As soon as he was grown enough, the long-legged boy decided he would leave and start a new life as a soldier. He thought this way he could become the warrior he dreamed of being. He thought a soldier's life would be adventurous and fun, and so he made ready to leave.

When the day arrived that the boy was to depart, his mother prepared a bag lunch for him and packed him an extra pair of socks. As he made his way toward the door, his father was silent, but his mother drew him aside and whispered these words:

My son, remember this and take it with you as you go: God wore a man's face, that we might look on Him always. If you are ever in need of help, you can always call on Him. He will never fail you but will hear you and help you in your time of need.

Yet there is one who lives in darkness, and you should shun him, for his home is the house of falsehood and his kingdom the realm of hell. Love the truth and turn your mind away from his lies, and don't waver between his ways and the ways of God, because the labor of one who wavers will always be in vain. My son, nothing comes easy. If you are to realize your dreams, you must be willing to work hard and serve others.

Thus, his mother embraced him and tearfully said goodbye, her words echoing in his ears.

Life as a Soldier

The long-legged boy tucked his mother's words far away in the back of his mind, not knowing that one day they

would come to hold great value for him. He joined the military and entered into soldiering with high expectations of adventure.

But it wasn't long before he grew tired of all the hard work that it took to become a soldier. He had to march for twenty miles with a heavy pack. He had to stand at attention for hours at a time. He had to crawl on his elbows across fields of rocks. And becoming a soldier required him to follow even more rules than when he lived at home:

- "Shine your shoes!"
- "Make your bed!"
- "Clean your weapon!"

As much as he liked the idea of becoming a mighty warrior, he didn't like the work it took to become one. He preferred the warrior life of his daydreams. And so, the long-legged boy decided he'd had enough.

No Rules

When his enlistment was up, the long-legged boy left the soldier's life and proceeded to live a life without rules. He did as he pleased. He stopped cutting his hair. He lived outdoors, mostly spending his time sitting on street corners playing his guitar. He didn't wash his clothes, he didn't eat peas, his shoes were not shined, and he stayed up as late as he wanted, free to spend the night under the stars wherever he found himself.

No matter how uncomfortable life became for the long-legged boy, at least no one told him what to do.

The Curly-Haired Girl

Not far away, in a bustling seaport town, lived a curly-haired girl. Exotic people came and went in the seaport town. They continually poured in by ship from all around the world, with their colorful costumes, unusual customs, and strange ideas. The curly-haired girl lived with her father and mother in a house where artists, musicians, and poets from all over the world were always hanging out at all hours of the day and night, loudly discussing the latest philosophies and topics of the day. It was like the circus was in town all the time at her home.

Amidst all the commotion, her parents were too busy focusing on their art and entertaining fascinating artist guests to care much for the curly-haired girl. So, she was left alone to care for herself. She was used to grabbing whatever she could find in the cupboard when she was hungry and deciding for herself when it was time to sleep or get up, what to wear, and how her time should be spent.

In fact, the curly-haired girl's parents raised her without any rules at all. She was allowed to do anything she pleased:

- She didn't have to make her bed.
- She could draw on the walls.
- She could eat pop-tarts for dinner.

But sometimes during the early evenings, she would leave her noisy house and wander through the streets. This was the time of day when quiet descended on the town, and households turned their attentions inward. She would stop and peer into the picture windows of houses not far from her home. There, she saw mothers and fathers with children, all sitting together around their dinner tables. Sometimes they bowed their heads in prayer before their meals. They all seemed so happy to be together as a family—so orderly and peaceful and caring. She wondered what it would be like to belong to such a family. It made her long for something she couldn't name.

Life as an Art Student

When she was old enough, the curly-haired girl left home to study art. As she was waiting for her bus to leave town, it happened that a lady passing by recognized her as that little neighbor girl who used to peer through her window and watch her family as they shared dinner.

"Where are you going?" the lady asked. "I'm on my way to art school," the curly-haired girl replied. "I'd like to tell you something," the lady said. She sat down next to her, drew in a slow breath, and began.

> ## "Remember this, child: there is One who watches over you and cares about you."

My daughter, for many years I have watched you and prayed for you. Remember this, child: there is One greater than me who watches over you and cares about you. He is the source of all that is good, and in your darkest hour of need, He will find you, make you His own, and give you a home where you belong.

But be sure to resist the evil one, for he is the one that lives in shadows and is the source of chaos. You can find order if you love truth, if you do all things with excellence, and if you give yourself over to serve others.

The curly-haired girl heard the lady's words and caring tone, but she didn't understand. Still, she tucked those words deep into her back pocket.

When she got to art school, the curly-haired girl found there were even fewer rules there than at home.

- She could stay up all night and never go to bed at all.
- She could spray-paint graffiti on the walls of big buildings.
- She could eat nothing but pop-tarts morning, noon, and night.

This freedom was very familiar and comfortable for her, and she enjoyed it. After finishing art school, the curly-haired girl continued doing exactly as she pleased, just as she had always done.

She made up her own rules, and most importantly, no one told her what to do.

The Curly-Haired Girl Meets the Long-Legged Boy

One day, the curly-haired girl was walking along when she heard the sound of music coming from down the street. She followed the sound to where she saw a skinny, lanky-haired boy playing guitar on a street corner. It was the

long-legged boy. He was a young man now, and she was becoming a young woman. She sat down beside him and listened to his song. She knew the song he was singing and began to sing along. With a sparkle in his eye, he said, "Hey, you sound pretty good!"

And from that moment on, the long-legged boy and the curly-haired girl spent every minute together. They shared a love of life without any rules.

They sang and played guitar from town to town. Sometimes they painted on walls. And they ate lots of pop-tarts and never ate peas. Together, they did whatever they wanted to do, without thought for where they were headed, the consequences of their actions, or who might get hurt. They ate what they wanted. They lived in a van. They left town when they felt like it. They drank and got high. And they got physically intimate even though they were not committed in marriage.

No Consequences

Certainly, it's a lot of fun to live by your own rules. But sometimes when people do whatever they want without thinking of where they're headed or the consequences of their actions or who might get hurt, bad things can happen.

Even good things like eating and travel and seeking happiness and physical intimacy can be harmful if you're not paying attention to consequences.

If people are hungry and they eat, that may be fine. But if they only eat pop-tarts, what happens then? If people want to travel,

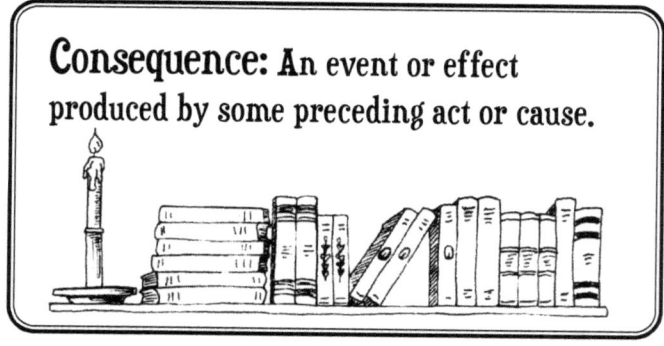

Consequence: An event or effect produced by some preceding act or cause.

that may be fine. But if they leave town without taking care of business—like unpaid parking fines or people who are counting on them—what happens then? If people seek happiness, that may be fine. But if they seek it by getting drunk and high, what happens then? If people get physically intimate but they are not in a committed marriage, what happens then?

What Happens Then?

That's the question: What happens when you do what you want without considering consequences? Maybe in math class you learned how to balance equations. All the numbers on one side of the equal sign have to have the same value as the number on the other side of the equal sign. What does math have to do with consequences? Life is like that. All actions have an equal and opposite reaction. To imagine that you can act and *not* be faced with the consequences of your actions is to live in a dream world. It's not reality.

The long-legged boy and curly-haired girl preferred their dream world to reality. They ate too many pop-tarts and left town too often and got drunk and high and got physically intimate without the commitment of marriage. And yes, there were consequences that the long-legged boy and the curly-haired girl had to face even though they didn't want to. There were unpaid parking fines. There were tummy aches. There were broken friendships. There were hangovers.

One Particular Consequence

But one consequence of their actions was particularly noteworthy. These two dim drifters didn't consider that one of God's designs for physical intimacy is that babies are made that way. And sure enough, a baby began to grow in the girl's womb—the growing place for a baby in her body. Because they were not in a committed marriage, and because they hated rules, they saw a baby as something that would get in the way of their life of fun and living only for themselves.

"I know what we'll do," said the girl. "We'll have the baby removed." When she was growing up in the bustling seaport town, the girl was told by everyone around her that when you had an unwanted baby in your belly, all you had to do was go to a special place and get rid of it—easy.

The boy was not thinking and readily agreed to the plan. He put out of his mind his child growing inside her, figuring that removing it was probably something like getting a tooth extracted. No big thing at all. And so, he stayed home in their van and plucked on his guitar while she took off for her appointment at that special place whose business it was to take care of such problems.

The "Problem" Removal

When she got to the office, the curly-haired girl began to have a strange feeling. The place seemed haunted, and she shivered without knowing why.

The people at that office told the girl, "Don't worry. You're doing the right thing. You're young and have your whole life ahead of you. We can take away this problem, and you can go right back to your life as though nothing ever happened. It won't hurt, and it will all be over in a minute. That will be $500 please."

> When she got to the office, the curly-haired girl began to have a strange feeling. The place seemed haunted, and she shivered without knowing why.

The girl paid the money and was seated with other girls in the waiting room. When her turn came to go into the private room in the back, she was in for a rude shock. She found that what they had told her was not the truth. Having the baby removed was very painful and difficult indeed. When it was all over, the girl started to cry in confusion and pain because she realized that the "problem" she had just removed was actually a tiny, growing person with a beating heart. She had made a big mistake.

After it was done, the people who worked in the office shuffled the curly-haired girl out the back door so the girls in the front waiting room wouldn't see or hear her cry—that might be bad for business. She tearfully descended the back stairs in confusion.

As she wandered away, she saw through her tears a colorful object directly in her path, there on the ground. She stopped and bent down to pick it up and held it before her face to see what it was. She wiped her tears and saw that it was an old coin with a message on it. She read the words, *"He careth for you."* Could this be a message meant just for her, just as the kind neighbor lady had spoken of—a message from the one who watched over her and cared about her even in her very darkest hour of need? Could that one care and love her in spite of her terrible failure?

We'll return to the story of the long-legged boy and the curly-haired girl later, but for now, let's see what we can learn from them.

Some questions for you:

1. How would you define the word *consequences*?

2. What is the purpose of rules?

3. Do you allow people to tell you what to do? How does that help you? How does that make your life harder?

Notes:

3 • Aiming toward the Good

What can we learn from these two characters—the long-legged boy and the curly-haired girl? They came from vastly different beginnings, had different sorts of parents, and grew up in different types of homes. But what they had in common was that they made their choices based on a me-centered view of life. Because of the choices they made, they suffered wounds from the enemy in that Great Battle—and they weren't even aware that they were in the battle.

If we were to give the long-legged boy a name, we might call him *Mr. Feel-Likit*. He made his choices based on whether he did or did not *feel like it*. He didn't *feel like* getting up early because it was much more comfortable to play his guitar in bed until noon. He didn't *feel like* having a job because he preferred the world of his dreams, where he was already very accomplished and didn't have to work for it. If that meant that he and his girl could only afford to live in a van, well at least in their van no one told them what to do. Having fun with his girl was more important than caring for others, so he didn't *feel like* thinking about the baby that only got in the way of his fun.

If we were to give the curly-haired girl a name, we might call her *Ms. Don-Wanna*. She chose not to do anything she didn't want to do for this simple reason: "*Don-wanna*." Ms. Don-Wanna *didn't wanna* do anything but scribble graffiti on walls and take selfies. She *didn't wanna* get dressed most days, so she just went around in pajamas and slippers, as she'd always been used to doing. She *didn't wanna* be burdened with a kid, so she didn't think too deeply about that person growing in her belly—that is, until it was too late.

Mr. Feel-Likit and Ms. Don-Wanna paid no attention to where their choices were leading them in life and who might get hurt along the way. They lived for "immediate gratification." What does that mean? It means getting everything you want *right now*, without working for it or having to wait or pause and think about where your choices will lead.

They didn't yet know that they had chosen a path—one that can lead to bad outcomes. Making bad choices meant they were losing in the Great Battle, and it had real consequences that could be seen and felt in their lives.

Mr. Feel-Likit and Ms. Don-Wanna couldn't see the patterns in their choices, but maybe you can. Where do you suppose their choices were leading them?

Another Way to Be

Now imagine a different pair of characters. We'll name them *Miss Ought-To* and *Mr. Do-Right*. These two make different choices and make them in a different way from Mr. Feel-Likit and Ms. Don-Wanna.

You see, inside of each of us is a voice that tells us what we ought to do and what we ought not to do, but not everyone pays attention to that voice. Miss Ought-To has learned to listen to that voice inside. She is aware of her place in the Great Battle and what sort of choices she needs to make for the best outcomes in her life. She knows that she *ought to* take responsibility for helping around the house, even if she doesn't feel like it. She *ought to* do her best at

> Inside of each of us is a voice that tells us what we ought to do and what we ought not to do, but not everyone pays attention to that voice.

work because anything less than the best is just not her style. She *ought to* stay away from the drugs others are taking because she values her sharp mind. She pays special attention to how she dresses, as she *ought to,* knowing that showing a bunch of skin gives confusing messages to boys and makes her feel like her only value is her body.

Miss Ought-To has learned—mostly by watching the heartbreaks her friends go through—that physical intimacy *ought to* be saved for committed marriage between a man and a woman who will stick by each other for their whole lives.

Mr. Do-Right also listens to that voice inside and knows he's in the Great Battle. He chooses to do things because they're the *right* thing to *do*. He refuses to use AI to write his assignments because it is *right* to be honest. He teaches math to the foster kids who live next door so they'll do better in school, because it's *right* to share your special talents with others who need help.

Mr. Do-Right treats his girlfriend with respect because it is *right* to value her for who she is, quite apart from his physical desires. He would never insult his girlfriend's honor by insisting on getting physically intimate with her before they marry. And since he isn't ready for marriage yet, he controls himself and behaves like a gentleman with her.

Miss Ought-To and Mr. Do-Right have jobs so they can contribute to their households and communities and not be a drain on others. People depend on them, and they get pleasure out of helping others. Can you see a pattern in the lives of these two? Where do you suppose their choices are leading them?

Lots of other men, women, boys, and girls are very similar to Mr. Feel-Likit, Ms. Don-Wanna, Miss Ought-To, and Mr. Do-Right. You may know people that fit these descriptions. We don't want to gossip so let's not name names—just observe and learn.

You can see that even if Mr. Feel-Likit and Ms. Don-Wanna don't know where they are aiming in life, they are aiming somewhere, and it is probably going to be a place of disappointment, failure, and low self-worth. You can see that Miss Ought-To and Mr. Do-Right are also aiming somewhere, and it is probably going to be a place filled with friendship, achievement, and self-respect.

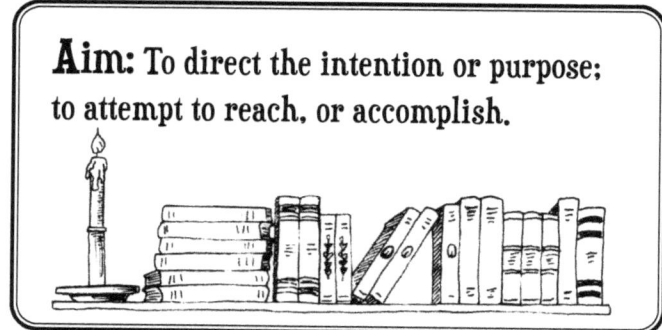

Aim: To direct the intention or purpose; to attempt to reach, or accomplish.

Aiming toward the Good

What do Miss Ought-To and Mr. Do-Right have in common? They both know they're in the Great Battle, and they know which side they're on: they're on the good side. They are skilled with their spiritual weapons because they continually practice aiming toward the good. Whether they are at their jobs, hanging out with friends, washing dishes, or just reading quietly by themselves, they are aiming toward the good. They choose to aim toward the good even when no one is looking. They choose to keep their thoughts from wandering away from the good. They may not always succeed, but the good is the target of every choice they make. And for you, whatever your plans are in life, aiming toward the good will help you make good choices and live your best life, too.

> **Whatever your plans are in life, aiming toward the good helps you make good choices and live your best life.**

Where you end up is a result of the choices you make. Every choice you make is either pointing you in the direction of bad outcomes or in the direction of good outcomes. Have you thought about where you want to end up? How can you learn to make good choices so you can get there? As we move along, we're going to answer these questions.

Some questions for you:

1. Do you know people like Miss Ought-To and Mr. Do-Right who inspire you to do what you *ought to do?*

2. Give an example of how a good choice you made led to a good outcome.

3. Give an example of how a bad choice you made led to a bad outcome.

4. In your own words, describe what it means to aim toward the good.

Notes:

4 • What Is the Good?

Now that we're talking about aiming toward the good, let's explore what exactly we mean by "the good." *Good* is not just some idea that somebody made up. No. It's not about random rules—it goes deeper than that. Good is the very nature of God. God is good, and he placed his moral compass within us so we can tell the difference between good and bad, right and wrong. I know this sounds heavy. Let's break it down.

Body, Mind, and Spirit

Human beings consist of body, mind, and spirit. We have bodies. Our bodies are made of flesh and blood. We need to eat and drink to stay alive, so we feel hunger and thirst. When we feel cold, we seek warmth. When we're tired, we sleep.

We also have minds. Our bodies tell our minds about our needs, and our minds make the choice of how to fill those needs. So, when we're hungry, our minds may choose for our bodies to go get something from the fridge or from the store or wherever that bodily need can be met.

Our minds make many choices throughout the day. "Should I get up early or late?" "Should I play video games before I do my homework?" "Should I help myself to a third donut?" In all these choices, our minds are at work.

But we humans are not only physical beings with minds. We are also spiritual beings, and the spiritual realm is where the idea of right and wrong lives. When we wrestle with a choice, such as whether to pay for our food at the store or to steal it, then our spirits inform our minds of the moral choice before us. We know that it is wrong to steal. How do we know? Our spirits hear God's moral voice. In this way, body, mind, and spirit work together. They are all part of who you are.

Gut Feelings

When you do something wrong, you get a feeling in your gut that tells you it is wrong. The sense of good and bad, right and wrong, ought to and ought not to, is right there inside of you.

> **A moral compass is sense of right and wrong that's planted deep inside of you.**

Picture a compass that points the way to true north. A *moral compass* is a sense of right and wrong that's planted deep inside of you. The way that is right is true north.

Think back to a time when you thought about doing something you knew was wrong. Your moral compass went to work alerting you—either with something like bright red flashing lights and noisy sirens or with something more like a gentle but persistent tap on your shoulder—to steer you away from wrong thoughts and actions and get you back on track aiming toward the good. Sometimes you listened. Sometimes you didn't. But you are equipped with this special tool to help you through life to make good choices and avoid bad ones. Learn to listen for it. It is your conscience.

Did you ever see that old Disney cartoon called *Pinocchio*? Jiminy Cricket was given the job of being Pinocchio's conscience. He sang this song:

Take the straight and narrow path,
and if you start to slide,
give a little whistle, give a little whistle,
and always let your conscience be your guide.

It's only a cartoon, but it gives good advice. Your God-given inner moral compass—your conscience—helps you aim toward the good. Let it be your guide.

"Good," the Big Little Word

We've been talking about aiming toward the good. You might think the word *good* is just a little word without much weight. So, you may say, "The pizza is good." "My day was good." "I have a good dog." But this word means much, much more. In fact, it is a *very big* little word.

Think about this: after completing each day of the creation of the universe, the Bible tells us that God said, "It is good." When He finished the whole creation project, he said it was *"very* good." You can see that God's idea of goodness is as big as the universe. Or maybe even bigger.

The good that God has in mind for you consists of, for example, the good air you breathe every day, the good food that nourishes your body so you can grow strong, your good mind for thinking and solving problems, your good opportunities to do things you love to do, and the good people in your life. The good is that you are alive and that God loves you, has countless blessings for you, and wants you in his family. God wants you to live your best life. You can see that *good* is really a very big word.

Who Gets to Decide What Is Good?

There would be no good without God because God is the author of good and the source of all that is good. When we aim toward the good, what we are saying is: "God, I recognize you as the author of good, and I trust you to know what is good for me."

On the other hand, when we do not care to aim toward the good, we are saying, "I don't want God's idea of what is good and bad, right and wrong. I prefer to decide that for myself." This is what the long-legged boy and the curly-haired girl said. They ignored the still, small voice of the moral compass inside of them because it got in the way of them doing what they wanted to do. In this way, they made themselves their own "gods." They made themselves a higher authority than God.

The Opposite of Good

Many others have made the same mistake. Let's go back to the very beginning of humanity. In the Bible, Adam and Eve decided they were better judges than God of what is good. God's enemy in the Great Battle—in this case showing up as a snake—encouraged them to make up their own rules about right and wrong. Adam and Eve wanted the fruit on a certain tree even though God had made it clear it was off-limits. They listened to the snake instead of God. This caused a break in Adam and Eve's relationship with God. It was as if they said, "No thanks, God. We don't like your rules. We'll make up our own rules based on what we want." This is where *sin* entered the picture and the Great Battle between good and evil began for all humankind.

What is sin? It is when we do what we know is wrong, like Adam and Eve did. The Bible tells us that our sin separates us from God.

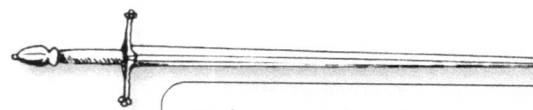

It is your sins that separate you from your God. He turns away from you when he sees them. (Isaiah 59:2)

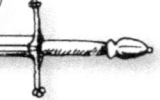

Ever since Adam and Eve, each child born has been the target of the evil one, just as Eve was. And just like that evil one wanted to destroy Adam and Eve, he has wanted to destroy every single person since then. There isn't anyone born who doesn't have to contend with the enemy of God. But as awful as that is, don't worry, because God has made a sure way to defeat that crafty enemy in the spiritual battle. We're going to learn about that later.

When we decide to make our own rules, we are no different from Adam and Eve. That's why their story is so important to understand the challenges we face in life. We all have an urge to do things our own way. But aiming toward the good helps keep us on a solid path. It's worth the effort because when we aim toward the good, we are aiming toward God.

Some questions for you:

1. Have you ever heard the voice of your inner, God-given moral compass speaking to you when you were making a choice?

2. Why does God get to define what is good?

3. What are some examples of the good that God has for you?

Notes:

5 • The Warrior's Mindset

When you decide you want to aim toward the good, you will need to prepare yourself for the battle. This is when you find out that aiming toward the good takes work. It's much easier to procrastinate, be lazy, let others do the hard stuff, and—basically—be a Mr. Feel-Likit or Ms. Don-Wanna. This is where the battle lines are drawn. To gain ground in the Great Battle, you must develop your warrior's mindset.

Many warriors throughout history have found it useful to join with others of like mind to serve a special purpose, such as protecting the weak and those less fortunate. They followed codes of conduct and took oaths that bound them together toward their common purpose. The codes ensured that they could trust each other in high-stress situations.

The codes of conduct that warrior groups develop come from a desire to follow a higher calling with a sense of honor and purpose. The warrior's mindset comes from a willingness to focus all efforts toward the good. Your willingness to aim toward the good will enable you to develop a warrior's mindset, too.

We find that the codes of conduct of many warrior groups through history and across the globe are similar. This similarity is because of the moral compass we talked about. It's part of who we are and how we are made. Let's let these few examples—in no particular order—of warrior groups and their codes of conduct inspire us.

The Marines

The United States Marine Corps is an elite American fighting force that is always the first into and the last out of the battlefield. These warriors of the U.S. military have a code of three core values they have been dedicated to since the very founding of the U.S.:

- **Honor:**

    The quality that empowers Marines to exemplify the ultimate in ethical and moral behavior: to never lie, cheat, or steal; to abide by an uncompromising code of integrity; to respect human dignity; and to have respect and concern for each other.

- **Courage:**

    The mental, moral, and physical strength ingrained in Marines that sees them through the challenges of combat and the mastery of fear, and to do what is right, to adhere to a higher standard of personal conduct, to lead by example, and to make tough decisions under stress and pressure.

- **Commitment:**

    Unrelenting determination to achieve a standard of excellence in every endeavor[1]

These core values exemplify the Marine both on the battlefield and off the battlefield. The Marine Corps motto is *semper fideles,* which means "always

---

1. "Marines: Values," mcipac.marines.mil/Staff-and-Sections/Special-Staff/ Civilian-Human-Resources-Office/About-the-Marine-Corps/Values/.

faithful." These warriors are always faithful and dedicated to completing their mission with honor, courage, and commitment.

The Samurai

The Japanese Samurai warrior of many centuries ago served the feudal barons of their day. They had a code of conduct called Bushido (literally "military-knight ways"), a way of life that built up the qualities of love of country, courage, mercy, gentleness, good manners, truthfulness, honor, and self-control. The Samurai warrior aimed toward these virtues: justice and rectitude, heroic courage, benevolence and compassion, respect, sincerity, honor, loyalty, and duty.

What is *rectitude?* When you hear that word, think of a soldier standing straight and tall, at attention. Rectitude means "moral integrity or righteousness." A famous Samurai warrior once said that rectitude is

> **A way of praising a Samurai was to say he was "a man without a me."**

the bone that gives firmness and stature. As without bones the head cannot rest on the top of the spine, nor hands move, nor feet stand, so without rectitude neither talent nor learning can make of a human frame a Samurai.[2]

A way of praising a Samurai was to say he was "a man without a me." This is a way of saying that considering the needs of others over one's own needs was the highest calling of the Samurai.

The Free Burma Rangers

Let's look at another group called the Free Burma Rangers (FBR). They are operating in the present day. The FBR is made up of people from many different races and nations that come together to help those living in war-torn nations

---

2. Alfred Stead, *Great Japan: A Study of National Efficiency* (London: John Lane, 1906), 45.

like Burma, Iraq, and Sudan. Their vision statement says they exist "to free the oppressed and to stand for human dignity, justice, and reconciliation." FBR shines a light on the actions of oppressors, reports human-rights abuses, and helps provide for people's needs—like medical care, clothing, shelter, and food. They work in some of the most dangerous war zones on earth, risking death and imprisonment every day to improve the lives of oppressed people.

The FBR has a code of ethics to guide the conduct of its members:

> *Love each other. Unite and work for freedom, justice, and peace. Forgive and don't hate each other. Pray with faith, act with courage, never surrender.*

Again, we see selflessness and a willingness to go through discomfort and risk to life just to help others.

The Guardian Angels

From war-torn nations we move to New York in the 1970s. Let's look at the code of the Guardian Angels. During the seventies, a crime wave took over New York City, and this group was founded to protect ordinary people from being preyed on by criminals who roamed the streets. The Guardian Angels value selflessly protecting the vulnerable, building community, acting with honesty, dependability, and compassionate problem-solving. Their founder said:

> *No one has the right to violate anyone's human rights or property. We are not going to tolerate it, and we've taken a solemn oath within the Guardian Angels to risk our lives and limbs to protect people that we don't even know.*[3]

The Guardian Angels wore red hats to set themselves apart. They rode the subways and patrolled rough neighborhoods. If you were on the street by yourself on some dark night and you spotted one of those red hats, you

---

3. Jim Coleman, "We Have Become Some of Their Worst Nightmares!" *Black Belt* (February 1988): 28–33.

knew you would be protected. They are still operating in many cities around the world today.

The Scouts

Scouts are trained up to be people of character. They have an oath, which is their code of conduct:

> *On my honor I will do my best to do my duty to God and my country and to obey the Scout Law; to help other people at all times; to keep myself physically strong, mentally awake, and morally straight.*

Here is that Scout Law they just mentioned:

> *A Scout is trustworthy, loyal, helpful, friendly, courteous, kind, obedient, cheerful, thrifty, brave, clean, and reverent.*[4]

The Medieval Knights

During the Middle Ages, the medieval knights pledged to honor a code of *chivalry* (a word that means "to be valiant," or heroic) to protect Christian pilgrims as they traveled to the Holy Land, as the pilgrims were vulnerable to attack by bandits.

Among other things, knights pledged the following[5]:

Succor: Aid; help; assistance; particularly, assistance that relieves and delivers from difficulty, want or distress.

---

4. Boy Scouts of America, "About the BSA," scouting.org/about/.

5. "Code of Chivalry," Medieval Life and Times, medieval-life-and-times.info/medieval-knights/code-of-chivalry.htm.

- To protect the weak and defenseless
- To give succor to widows and orphans
- To refrain from giving offense
- To obey those in authority
- To stay away from unfairness, meanness, and deceit
- To keep faith in God
- To speak the truth and be faithful to your word
- To be generous and give to everyone
- To finish what you start
- To respect the honor of women
- Not to shrink before your enemy
- To love the country where you were born

Ladies and Gentlemen

Have you ever wondered what it means to be a lady or a gentleman? Those words seem like relics from a time gone by. But they refer to the admirable qualities that help us aim toward the good. One of the dictionary definitions of the word *lady* is: "a woman of refinement and gentle manners." As for a *gentleman,* we read that he is "a man whose conduct conforms to a high standard of propriety or correct behavior."

For many who live according to a high standard of behavior, noble conduct is no less than an obligation. This standard of behavior is sometimes known by its French name: *noblesse oblige,* meaning "nobility obligates." It is the obligation to act honorably and be generous to others less fortunate than oneself.

In Jewish culture, a man or woman of integrity and honor is referred to as a *mensch.* This word literally means "man," or "person," but it has a deeper meaning: A mensch is simply the height of what manhood and womanhood are meant to be. A mensch is kind, compassionate, self-disciplined, merciful, respectful, trustworthy, and fair to all, acting out of a sense of obligation or duty to "uphold ideals of justice, mercy, prudence, and wisdom."[6]

Patriotism

You may have noticed that loving your country appears in more than one of the codes we looked at. Loving your country means being a patriot. As a patriot, you agree to abide by a special unspoken contract—that is, you will do your part to add to the common good as a contributing member of your community. By doing this, you are choosing to participate in something larger than yourself. This is true all over the world, no matter where you happen to be a citizen.

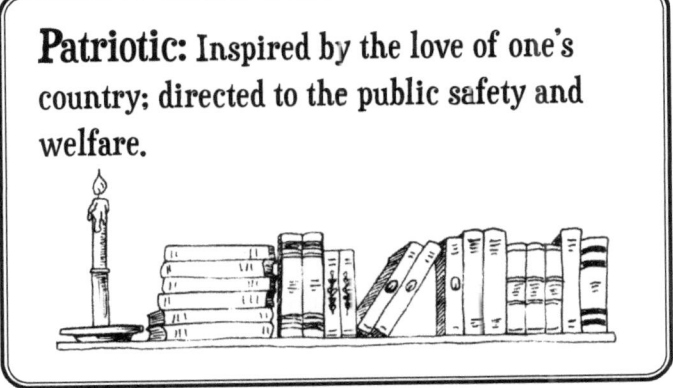

Patriotic: Inspired by the love of one's country; directed to the public safety and welfare.

But if you are a citizen of the United States of America, you are participating in the greatest self-government experiment in all of history. The U.S. was formed unlike any other nation in history. It was founded on a bold, new idea, not on race or ethnic heritage. All people are welcome to pledge their allegiance to the American experiment.

The bold idea behind the founding of the U.S. is that God is head of all, and below God are human beings, and then, below human beings is government—in that order. The rights enjoyed by American citizens come directly from God, and the stated purpose of government is to secure and protect those rights. The power exercised by the government comes only from the consent of the people. The rights spelled out in our Bill of Rights are all defined in the negative, meaning they are meant to forbid the government from acting against the individual's rights—not to confer positive rights, which is the domain of God alone.

---

6. Ronald Pies, *Becoming a Mensch: Timeless Talmudic Ethics for Everyone* (Lanham, MD: Hamilton Books, 2011), vi.

Before the founding of the U.S., all rights were given by governments and so could be taken away by governments. God-given rights cannot be taken away. This is what is meant by the term "inalienable rights," or rights that cannot be transferred to another. Our rights belong to all U.S. citizens. Among all the nations of the world, America is exceptional in this way. This is what is called "American exceptionalism."

> **Regardless of your national identity, your love of your country is what develops your patriotism, and loving your country will make you an asset wherever you live.**

Being a patriot means educating yourself about your government and the issues of the day. When you reach voting age, your vote can help protect your country from forces seeking to undermine it.

America's founders and patriots over the centuries have treasured the wonderful American idea to the point that they have been willing to shed their blood and even give their lives to establish and preserve it. By being a contributing member of society, you are taking your place among many brave patriots who have gone before you.

Regardless of your national identity, your love of your country is what develops your patriotism, and loving your country will make you an asset wherever you live.

Back to You

So, summarizing all these wonderful examples of codes of conduct, we can say that whenever you...

- are loyal, respectful, or helpful
- are honest and keep your word

- love your country
- care more about fairness than getting your share
- are mannerly, thoughtful, and kind
- protect the weak
- care more about lifting people up than tearing them down
- hold your tongue rather than speak ugly words

…then you are embodying the warrior's mindset and living out the heritage of the Marines, the Samurai, Free Burma Rangers, Guardian Angels, Scouts, medieval knights, ladies and gentlemen, and mensches. You are helping to improve the world around you. You are holding up your end of the bargain as a good citizen. You are aiming toward the good.

In the next chapter, we're going to introduce a code of conduct for you. Rather than a long list of items in your code, we're going to keep it really simple—just three items to tuck into your toolbelt to focus your attention on developing the warrior's mindset.

Some questions for you:

1. Which warrior group in this chapter inspired you the most?

2. What does it mean to embody the warrior's mindset?

3. What makes the United States of America unique?

Notes:

6 • Your Code of Conduct

We took a look at some inspiring codes of conduct. Now we're going to condense them into just three simple items to make a code of conduct for you:

- "I love truth."
- "I pursue excellence."
- "I serve others."

These three qualities can form a solid foundation as you learn to aim toward the good. Even though there are only three items listed here, they will be very challenging. They can give you a sense of purpose and focus. As people around you see you reaching for these qualities, they will come to trust that you are learning to be a person of integrity—one they can depend on.

As we discuss these three qualities, you will find a story to go along with each of them. Instead of stories about extraordinary warriors, these stories feature ordinary people aiming toward the good in their own personal ways.

Loving Truth

What is *truth*?

- **TRUTH: Purity from falsehood; honesty; sincerity; practice of speaking truth; conformity to fact or reality; exact accordance with that which is, or has been, or shall be.**

Loving truth means that you are honest with yourself and others, even if the truth is hard to face. It means hating lies. Loving truth touches on your actions, your character, and the words that come out of your mouth. Loving truth also means living in reality and facing up to the facts rather than hiding behind pretense or wishful thinking.

Here's a story about loving truth: Brianna liked to look good. She never left the house without making sure every hair was in place, her makeup was impeccable, and all her accessories matched to perfection. One day, Brianna stood in front of the open door of her closet and stared, wondering what to wear. In amongst the many outfits, she saw a dress she had forgotten about. Her uncle had sent her birthday money, and she had bought this little treat for herself.

Yet that was months ago, and she had never worn the dress. Now that she was reminded of it, she thought it was just right for hanging out with her friends in the patio area of the Starbucks. There

"Better not to ask permission," Brianna reasoned, "because Mom might say no."

was a new boy who had just started to join her friends that met there, and she was eager to make a good impression.

After Brianna put on this dress, she remembered why it had stayed in the closet for so long. Oh yeah, she didn't have any earrings to match it. That was so frustrating! She just didn't have what she needed to complete her look.

That was when Brianna remembered that her mother had a pair of earrings that would match perfectly. Without making a sound, she tip-toed into her mother's room, quietly opened her jewelry drawer, and found the earrings. She could have asked her mother permission to wear the earrings, but she knew that these earrings were special. They were a gift from her mom's mom. "Better not to ask permission," Brianna reasoned, "because Mom might say no." So Brianna slipped the earrings into her pocket and didn't tell a soul.

Brianna always got compliments on her appearance, and that made all the time in front of the mirror worthwhile. This time was no different. She had a great time with her friends and sensed that the new boy was at least a little bit interested in her. She was looking her best, and that was all that mattered.

After a few hours, the boys left and only the girls remained. Her ears started to get sore from the earrings, so she took them off and set them beside her on the table. The girls were singing loudly to all the cars as they slowly made their way through the drive-thru, which was right next to the patio area. That was so entertaining! People gave them the funniest looks as they drove by!

Brianna had some homework to do that night, so she finally said goodbye to her friends and headed home. When she got home, she changed into her sweats and slippers and began to relax. Suddenly, with a jolt, she remembered her mother's earrings. She scoured her purse and pockets, but the earrings were not there. Now she didn't care how she looked—she just sped back to the Starbucks as quickly as she could and searched around the patio area. She asked at the checkout counter. She tore through their lost-and-found box. She interrogated the barristas. She called her friends. No earrings. Brianna's heart sank.

Maybe her mother wouldn't notice the earrings were gone. Maybe Brianna just wouldn't admit what she'd done. No one would know who took them. This seemed like a good plan for awhile, but eventually it wore her out. After that day, no matter how pretty she made herself, she felt dirty and ugly because of her secret. She was so ashamed of herself.

Finally, Brianna came up with a plan. She took her small allowance and went to WalMart. She found the prettiest pair of earrings that a few dollars could buy. It made her sad that the only earrings she could afford were these cheap things, while her mother's earrings had been precious. But she just hoped this effort would make some difference.

Later that day, Brianna confessed to her mother what she had done. With tears, she asked her mother to forgive her and presented her with the new earrings. Her mother was disappointed. There was an uncomfortable silence that lasted a long, long time. Finally, her mother smiled softly and forgave Brianna, thanking her for her honesty and efforts to replace what was lost.

Brianna's mother missed her special earrings, but she had new earrings that she loved to wear even more because they reminded her of her daughter's love of truth. And whenever Brianna saw her mother wearing those earrings, she remembered how good it felt to be forgiven and loved in spite of her mistakes. Telling the truth had its rewards.

Pursuing Excellence

What is *excellence*?

• **EXCELLENCE: The state of possessing good qualities in an unusual or eminent degree; the state of excelling in any thing. . . . Purity of heart, uprightness of mind, sincerity, virtue, piety, are excellencies of character.**

A life of pursuing excellence is a life of diligently pushing yourself to do all things with unusual care, as though you were doing them for God himself. No room for less than your best.

Once there was a young man wandering around the New York City streets with a violin under his arm. He finally stopped and asked a policeman, "Sir, how do I get to Carnegie Hall?" (Carnegie Hall is in New York City. It is the most prestigious concert hall in the world, and only the best musicians can play there.) Seeing the violin, the policeman smiled and replied, "Practice! Practice!"

This funny little tale points out an important truth, which is that in order to achieve excellence, you need to practice at it—work hard. It doesn't come for free. By creating good habits and practicing them, you can excel in your pursuits. Now here's a real story about the pursuit of excellence:

> **Jen could have turned up her nose at a cleaning job. She could have said, "I'm too good for that."**

Jen was all about her children. When she wasn't homeschooling them, she was making their meals, planning their outings, shopping for them, and doing the many things that go into managing a household with lots of kids. But during COVID, things changed for Jen's family, and she had to find work to help her husband cover all the household expenses.

By chance, a local church needed someone to clean their building every week before services. Jen could have turned up her nose at a cleaning job. She could have said, "I'm too good for that." Instead, she took the job and took the opportunity to pursue excellence in her job performance.

This meant that she had to get up at 4 a.m. in order to get the job done and return home before her kids woke up at 7:30. As it turned out, one of her children began to wake up every time she got ready to leave in the early hours of the morning. This was George. Because Jen had to get her work done, she started taking George with her. At first, he napped on the church pews. But one day, he watched his mother as she scrubbed the toilets, put away the toys where the little ones had made messes in the Sunday-school rooms, scraped gum off the carpets, changed paper-towel rolls, and dusted window sills. It looked like fun!

"Mom, can I help you work?" Jen was delighted by George's helpful attitude. She taught him to do all her tasks and to do them with excellence.

Once a month, this church gave over its fellowship hall to house the homeless for a night. After those overnights, sad to say, the toilets were particularly challenging to get clean. Yet, George saw his mother's determination to do even the yucky jobs with excellence. Learning from her example, it seemed like the harder the task, the more positive was George's attitude.

George got a lot of satisfaction—not only from how he was appreciated for his hard work but from knowing he gave his best efforts, no matter how lowly the job (plus he always got a breakfast burrito on the way home). What gave him the most satisfaction was the feeling that he was cleaning Jesus's house, and George would do nothing less than his best for Jesus.

You can see that if you develop the habit of bringing excellence to all you do, then even the most menial or even unpleasant task will be a source of self-respect for you and an example to others. Excellence becomes its own reward.

Serving Others

What is *service*?

- **SERVICE: When you do something for another's benefit, which promotes interest or happiness.**

Serving others goes against the urge to think of yourself first. It requires thoughtful consideration and builds your character by making you alert to the needs of those around you instead of just keeping your focus on your needs alone. People who serve others are a great benefit to the world around them. They promote happiness.

Luke had just gotten his driver's license. He loved his new independence, and he looked forward to showing off his driving in front of his friends. Luke went to church on Sunday mornings with his family, but there was plenty of time afterwards to do what he wanted.

Luke's idea of the perfect Sunday afternoon was to have all his buddies pile into the car and go to the park to play touch football. When they were done with football, the best spot to just hang out and talk and laugh was wherever his car was parked. They would do that until the sun went down on Sunday evening. It seemed like the whole world revolved around Luke's car.

> ## It seemed like the whole world revolved around Luke's car.

There was an elderly member of the church where Luke attended who was recently widowed. With the passing of her husband, she no longer had a way to get to church on her own. This was brought to Luke's attention by the church staff. They asked Luke, "Are you willing to help out Sister Rusher by giving her a ride on Sundays?" Luke didn't give much thought to what this would mean to his after-church plans. He just said yes because he saw there was a need that he could fill. He agreed to pick her up and take her home every Sunday.

Luke got up extra early Sundays so he could go out of his way to pick up Sister Rusher and get them both to church on time. He carefully walked

her to her seat—the same seat way down near the front she and her husband had occupied for forty years. After church services, Sister Rusher seemed to take forever to leave. She walked very slowly, and she stopped often to chat with her many old friends. This was her only time during the week to socialize with others. She liked to get a donut and a cup of tea from the hospitality table.

On the way home, Sister Rusher often asked if Luke minded stopping to pick up a prescription at the pharmacy or a dozen eggs from the market. This meant that often, there was no time left at all to play football with his friends. This wasn't exactly what Luke first imagined having a car would be all about.

One day, it was like a lightbulb went off in Luke's head. He suddenly realized that he was needed, and it felt good. His car was a tool that could help people. He liked the idea of helping people even if it meant being late to his football games. From that time on, many people who needed rides ended up in Luke's car. He earned a reputation as the one who said yes with a smile.

Putting It All Together

Loving truth, pursuing excellence, and serving others require a lot of practice. It may help if you take note of when you see these qualities in others. Did someone let you go ahead of them in line at the store? Did a family member leave you the last dinner roll because they knew you wanted it? Did someone pick up after you at the crafts table? Did a friend correct himself when he started to exaggerate the truth? Let these be examples for you. If you look for opportunities, you will find ways to practice your code, starting small and gradually working up to bigger ways.

> Your choices will be those that come from a heart that loves truth, pursues excellence, and serves others.

With your code of conduct as your guide, you will find that it is easier to make good choices in any given situation. Which choice best honors truth, allows you to do your best, and helps someone? Your choices will be those that come from a heart that loves truth, pursues excellence, and serves others. Your code is a clear way of aiming you toward the good, and it benefits the world around you and sets a good example for others. And that will benefit you in the long run.

Following your code will stretch and challenge you to act in ways that may not feel familiar. Bravo to you for trying new things! In time, you will see the results of this new way of making choices. You might wish to keep a journal of the little ways (and the big ways!) you follow your code, and what the results are. Remember that practice makes perfect.

Some questions for you:

1. Are you willing to sign on to this code of conduct and call it your own?

2. Can you think of a time when someone you know showed a love of truth?

3. Can you think of a time when someone you know showed pursuit of excellence?

4. Can you think of a time when someone you know showed service to others?

Notes:

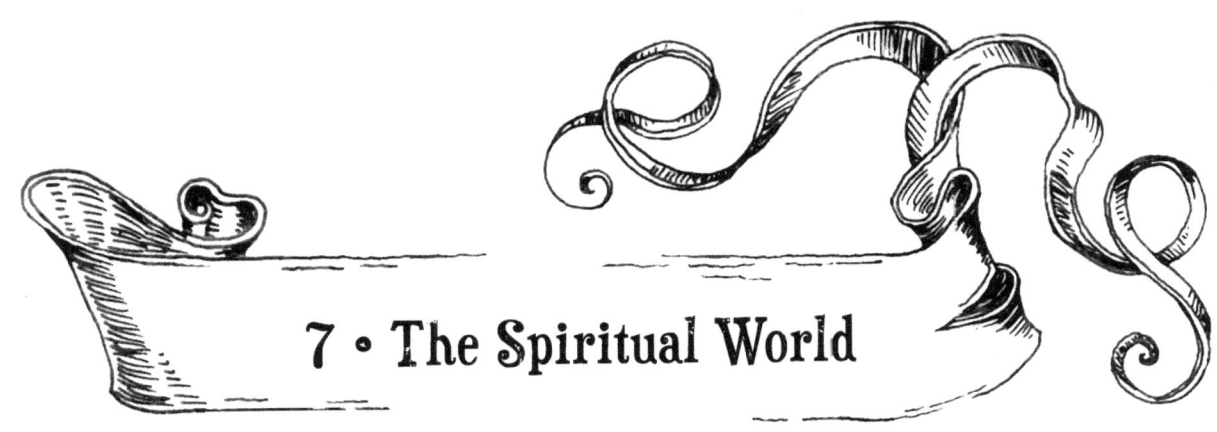

7 • The Spiritual World

You're young, with so much ahead of you. You may have a career one day. Your world may include adventure and travel. Or maybe you're gifted with creative business ideas. Perhaps you want to develop your physical strength and excel in sports. Or maybe you have artistic talent.

Then there are your personal relationships. Friendship offers the joy of companionship and being with people who think like you and who challenge you. For many of you, marriage and parenthood are part of your future. No doubt, as you step into adulthood, your life will be full of surprises. These are all wonderful pursuits in the physical world.

But your life is not just about what goes on in the physical world. It's also about what goes on in the spiritual world. The spiritual world is a *whole nother* way of experiencing life.

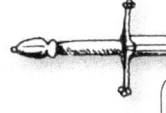

What we see lasts only a short time, and what we cannot see will last forever. (2 Corinthians 4:18)

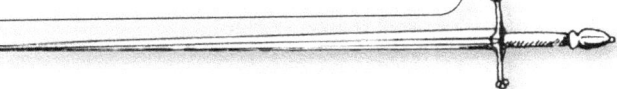

What is this spiritual world? While the world we see around us lasts only a short time, the spiritual world exists outside of time. It is forever. It is even more important than career, adventure, friendship, sports, money, and even the most wonderful worldly things. The spiritual world is where we encounter God.

Who Is God?

God has revealed himself to us through his Word—that is, the Holy Bible. It's impossible to say all that God is, but let's start with some basics. The Bible tells us that God is the Creator of the universe and the source of all life. He is infinite in knowledge, power, and all that is holy and good. He is perfectly just and righteous. He knows us inside and out because he created us. As immense as God is, he cares about you and me.

We can think of God as having three "persons," Father, Son, and Holy Spirit—one God in three parts. This is called the Trinity. Imagine a single jewel. It is one, yet, when you turn it, you see different facets, or faces. But it is still one jewel. This is just an example of the three-in-one idea. So it is with God in three persons. Each of the three in the Trinity has a unique facet, yet they are all one and in harmony with each other.

God the Father is that person of the Trinity that is the source and Creator of all things. He is not visible to us, but we see his creation around us every day. Although God is beyond our full understanding, we can relate to him as a loving father.

God the Son, Jesus Christ, is that person of the Trinity that took the form of a person and came to live on earth. His teachings, exemplary life, and sacrifice all show his great love for us.

Exemplary: Serving for a pattern or model for imitation; worthy of imitation.

God the Holy Spirit is the Spirit of Jesus and the Father, living in the hearts of those who believe in God. The Holy Spirit guides us into all truth and acts as our conscience, helps and comforts us, and points us to Jesus.

The Kingdom of God

The kingdom of God, sometimes called the kingdom of heaven, is not an imaginary fairy-tale kingdom of castles and moats and dragons and dragon slayers—though, like the imaginary fairy-tale kingdom, it is set apart from the physical world. The kingdom of God is not designed by human architects or constructed by human hands, of brick, cement, glass, or steel—though, like the human-made world, it is real. God is its architect and builder. You can't journey to this kingdom on horseback or by train or rocket or on foot. Siri and Alexa can't give you directions.

The kingdom of God is not on any map, yet it is no less real than all around us that we can see and touch. Think about love. Love is another example of something we can't see and touch, yet we know it's real and very powerful.

Jesus spent a lot of time teaching when he was on earth. We can learn a lot about God's kingdom from Jesus's words. Let's just focus on one such teaching. Here's what Jesus said:

The Kingdom of Heaven is like a merchant on the lookout for choice pearls. When he discovered a pearl of great value, he sold everything he owned and bought it! (**Matthew 13:45-46**)[1]

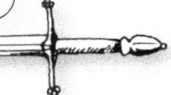

This description of the kingdom of heaven does not make any sense in the physical world, which gives us a fantastic opportunity to practice seeing things with spiritual eyes. The important thing to notice about this teaching is that Jesus describes the kingdom not as a place but as a person—one actively on the lookout for fine pearls. He finds a pearl that is so choice that he sells everything he owns to buy it. That must have been one

---

1. New Living Translation. (These notes tell you what Bible version the Scripture quote came from. If there is no note, the quotes came from the Easy-to-Read Version.)

extraordinary pearl! Can you think of an object for which you would go and sell all that you have just to own it?

Guess what. In this teaching about the kingdom of God, you can think of Jesus as the merchant and you as that pearl of great value. Yes, Jesus considers you of such high value that he spent all he had—his very life—to purchase you.

In God's kingdom, you are valued and loved for who you are. The kingdom of God is a kingdom of perfect love, and that love is available to you. Here is how the Bible describes God's perfect love:

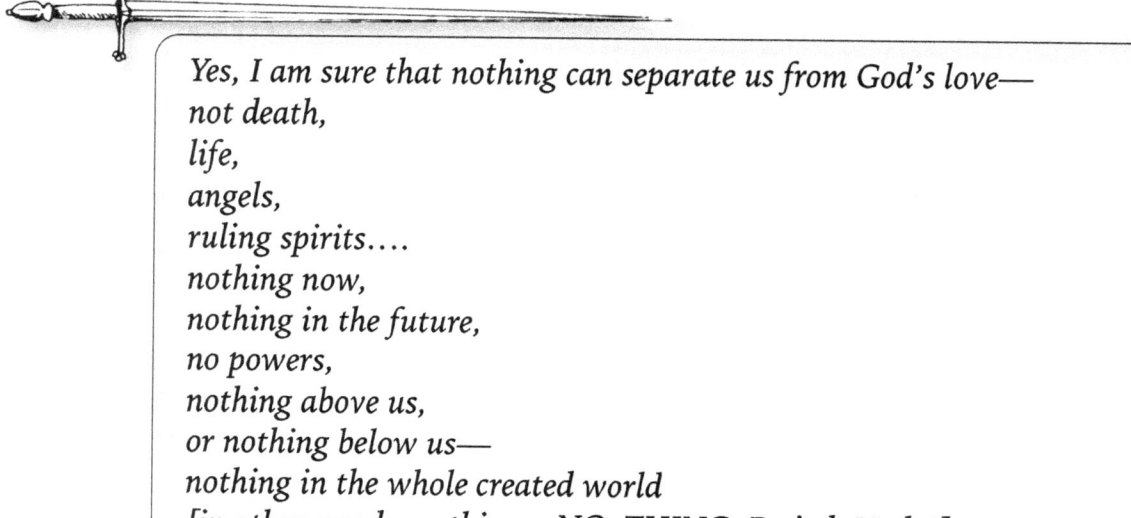

Yes, I am sure that nothing can separate us from God's love—
not death,
life,
angels,
ruling spirits....
nothing now,
nothing in the future,
no powers,
nothing above us,
or nothing below us—
nothing in the whole created world
[in other words, nothing—NO. THING. Period. Nada!]
—will ever be able to separate us from the love God has shown us in
Christ Jesus our Lord.
(Romans 8:38-39)

Who Am I?

Jesus says you're a pearl of great value. But maybe you're not so sure of who you are. As you mature, you begin to question your identity. "Who am I?" You hear the words people say about you, and you add them to the image you see in the mirror to form a picture in your mind of who you think you are. But is that really who you are?

Many times, the things people say about us are far from the truth. They may even be cruel words meant to make us feel small. Also, we're busy comparing ourselves to others, so our view of ourselves is distorted. The question is, Where can we find a true picture of who we are?

> *So God created humans in his own image. He created them to be like himself. He created them male and female. God blessed them.*
> (Genesis 1:27-28)

This is where your true identity comes from. Your true worth is defined by God's great love for you.

God made human beings in a unique way. Unlike all the rest of his creation, he made us *in his image*. This is a great privilege he gave to us, to be the carriers—the ambassadors—of his image. As such, every single person possesses great dignity and worth in his eyes, including you.

Many times, the message given by society—social media, your school, movies, books, and music—goes against this idea of the inherent, God-given dignity of human life. This is why you see people treating themselves and others as though they have no value. Those others might even include the unborn, which are too often treated as trash instead of as precious children of God. Or very old people, who are sometimes encouraged to "get out of the way." Perhaps you know people who cut themselves or have eating disorders or other self-destructive behaviors, even as extreme

as thinking about taking their own lives. Many have believed a lie about who they are. They believe they have no value.

But they do have value in God's eyes, and so do you. You have great value precisely because you are God's precious and beloved child. This is where your true identity comes from. Your true worth is defined by God's great love for you. He found you so worthy of his love that he laid down his life for you.

> This is real love—not that we loved God, but that he loved us and sent his Son as a sacrifice to take away our sins. (**1 John 4:10**)[2]

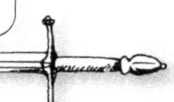

> # If you've ever wished you were loved with perfect love, that was you longing to be with God and to be embraced by his perfect love.

Once you see yourself with the value you have in God's eyes, you will see yourself as you truly are. You are the beloved.

Perfect Love

We just talked about a kingdom in which you are so valuable, just like that precious pearl, that Jesus gave his life for you. We described how God's love for you is what his kingdom is all about. His love is unlike love that comes from anywhere else. It is beyond the love your mother, your father, your friends, your brother and sister, or your grandparents can give you. They may love you a lot, but their love is human—that means imperfect.

Perhaps you know something about imperfect love. One person who was

---

2. New Living Translation.

supposed to love you perfectly was thinking only of herself. Another person who was supposed to love you perfectly didn't listen. Another wasn't fair. And another was abusive. We've all seen how human love can fall short. You may have been on the receiving end of imperfect love, and you may have given imperfect love, too.

God's love doesn't suffer from human imperfection. God's love is beyond human measure. His love is perfect. Maybe nobody has ever told you before of your great value. God wants you to know that you have the highest value in his eyes. Maybe you never thought about being with God, much less desiring to be with Him. But if you've ever wished you were loved with perfect love, that was you longing to be with God and to be embraced by his perfect love. He placed that hunger for perfect love inside of you, knowing that only he can provide it, to draw you to him.

Yes, he humbled you by letting you go hungry and then feeding you.
(Deuteronomy 8:3)[3]

The Royal Law

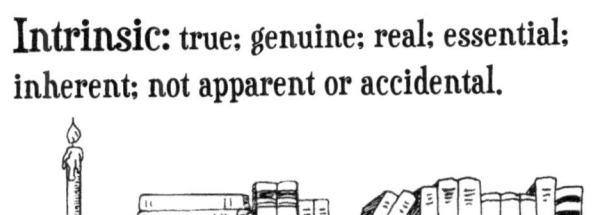

Intrinsic: true; genuine; real; essential; inherent; not apparent or accidental.

Let's take this to another level. Once you are able to see your intrinsic value, that will change the way you see others and their value. You will come to treat others with the same respect that God has for you. This brings us to what is called the "royal law" of Jesus,[4] and it goes like this:

---

3. New Living Translation.

4. James 2:8.

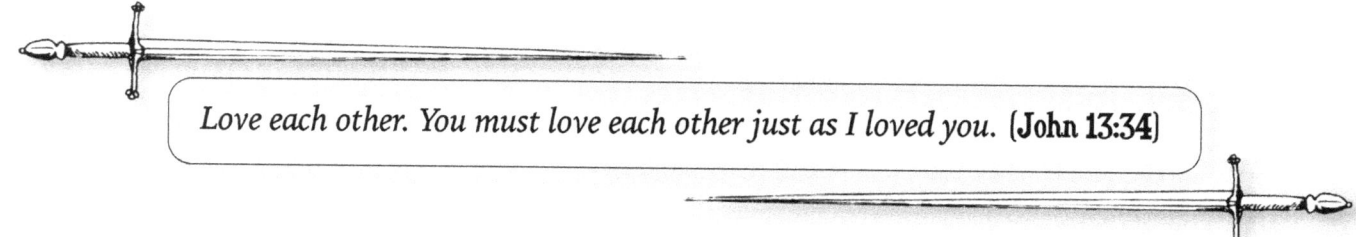

Love each other. You must love each other just as I loved you. (John 13:34)

God thinks so highly of you that he made you in his image. Just as you might resemble your grandfather or your auntie, you have a family resemblance to God. By loving others, you show that you are part of his family because he loves others, too. This is one way you show your love for God. It is also part of aiming toward the good.

You will find it is easy to love the loveable and difficult to love the unloveable and those who don't love you. This is where your code comes into play in the spiritual world. With difficult people, you can practice loving the truth—that is, the truth of how highly God values them, just as he values you. And you can practice serving them with excellence as a way to obey the royal law.

Some questions for you:

1. What are some of your life goals?

2. What does it mean to you that God made you in his image?

3. Where does your value come from?

4. What does it mean to you that God made even the people you don't like in his image?

Notes:

8 • Your Code Meets the Kingdom

Now that we've learned about the kingdom of God, let's return to the three qualities that make up your code of conduct: loving truth, pursuing excellence, and serving others. We know they help you in the physical world. Now we'll see how they help you on the spiritual side. We'll take them one at a time:

Truth in the Kingdom

Our *love of truth* is a way to say to God, "God, I will be honest with myself and with you. You see me inside and out. I have no secrets from you. I will be a person of integrity, even when no one is looking."

But love of truth goes much deeper than that. Jesus said *he is the truth*.

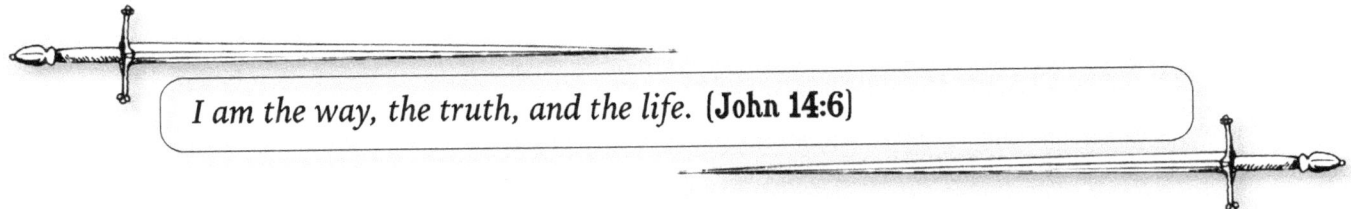

I am the way, the truth, and the life. (John 14:6)

What did Jesus mean by saying he is the truth? He meant that he embodies truth. Everything Jesus says and does is real, based in reality, genuine, and without deception, hidden motives, or trickery. He is what he says he is and

> **He is what he says he is and can be trusted to keep his word and never change in his character.**

can be trusted to keep his word and never change in his character. We can trust his words in the Bible because we know it isn't in his nature to lie. When we believe in Jesus, we are believing what is true.

But there is one who is the father of lies. He is the opposite of the truth. He is full of deceit. He offers you a counterfeit in place of the truth. What he offers may look pleasing, but it always has a hook in it. For example, the long-legged boy and curly-haired girl got "happy" with the use of drugs and alcohol, but it was not true happiness. It was a counterfeit offered by the enemy. Jesus offers joy, which is the true experience of deep, lasting happiness in life. Those two lost that round of the battle because they chose the counterfeit instead of the true.

Excellence in the Kingdom

Our *pursuit of excellence* is a way to say to God, like George did, "God, I'm going to do everything—whether it's my schoolwork, chores, or helping a stranger—as though I am doing it for you." This makes every task a spiritual act of worship.

> *Whatever you do, work at it with all your heart, as though you were working for the Lord and not for people.* (Colossians 3:23)[1]

---

1. Good News Translation.

Service in the Kingdom

Our *serving others* is a way to say to God, "God, I want to be more like you. You came to serve and not to be served." Jesus could have come as a mighty king, but instead he chose to humble himself—even to the point of dying on the cross. We are invited to lay our lives aside for others just as he did.

> The Son of Man [that's Jesus] came not to be served but to serve others and to give his life as a ransom for many. (**Mark 10:45**)[2]

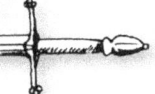

By considering the spiritual side of your code, you turn your attention to God. This adds meaning, purpose, and direction to all you do. It brings you out of the terrible loneliness of me-centered thinking into a partnership with God, where your actions have meaning and you are never alone.

Destination: The Kingdom

So, how do you get into this kingdom of God if it's not in the physical world? Aiming toward the good is great, but the problem is, there isn't a single person on earth who has ever been able to do that perfectly. We all struggle to do the right thing. It doesn't come naturally. We mess up. That is part of what it means to be human. Remember that baby who thought she was the center of the universe? A part of her is still that selfish baby, even as she grows and learns to behave like an adult.

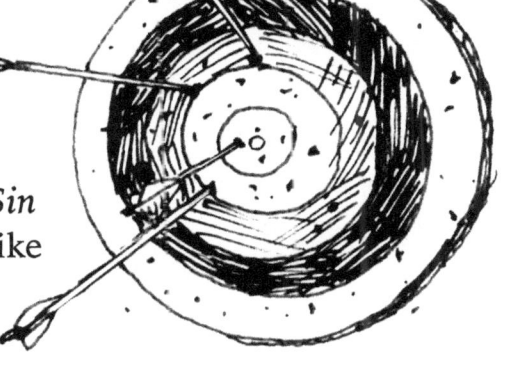

Another word for our mess-ups is *sin*. Sin is a word that means "missing the mark," like when the archer misses the bull's-eye on the target. Even if he just barely missed the

---

2. New Living Translation.

bull's-eye—still, he missed. Even if we do good 99 percent of the time, we still fail that 1 percent.

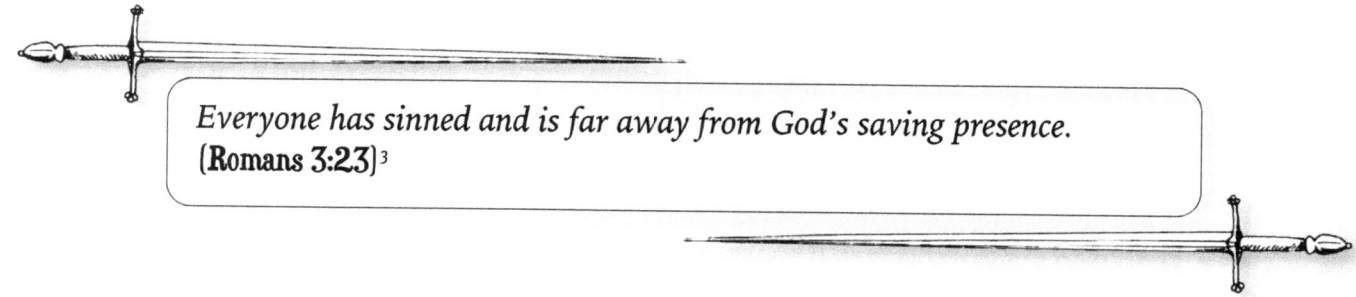

Everyone has sinned and is far away from God's saving presence. (Romans 3:23)[3]

We can't enter into the kingdom of God with sin in us because God is a holy God, and his kingdom is a holy place. There can be no sin in his presence.

But God

So, is that the end of the story? Too bad for you? No! God knows about your sin. He knows every time you've pinched your sister or stolen something from the store, every hateful thought in your head, every lie, and even all the way-worse stuff you may already be doing and may do in the future. He knows you intimately.

There is no way you can come into his kingdom with your sin because God is a just God and justice must reign in his presence. But still, God wants you to be with him in his kingdom. *So, he made a way.* He sent his Son, Jesus. What would you think if you did something really, really bad and instead of being punished for it, a perfect stranger stepped up and said, "Don't punish this one. I'll take the punishment instead." That's what Jesus did. He paid the highest price. He gave his life for your sins when he died on the cross.

Remember, the merchant was willing to sell everything he had to buy that pearl of great value. Jesus was willing to give everything he had so you, his precious pearl, could enter his kingdom. He purchased you.

---

3. Good News Translation.

We just said that there isn't a single person on earth who has ever been able to aim toward the good perfectly. But Jesus is the exception. He *is* the one and only person in human history who never sinned. Jesus always aims toward the good, and he always hits the bull's-eye. He is qualified to take all your sins on himself so that you can be free and enter his kingdom. It took one who was perfect to accomplish this—no one else could do it. He exchanged his perfection for your sinfulness:

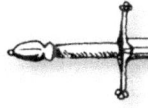

> *God made Christ, who never sinned, to be the offering for our sin, so that we could be made right with God through Christ.* (2 Corinthians 5:21)[4]

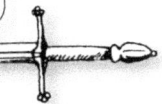

What do you have to do to enter into God's kingdom? It's amazingly simple. All you have to do is believe:

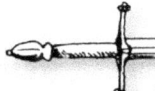

> *Yes, God loved the world so much that he gave his only Son, so that everyone who **believes in him** would not be lost but have eternal life.* (John 3:16)

Jesus lived out the code of truth, excellence, and service necessary to complete his mission of being the perfect sinless sacrifice for our sin. For all sister-pinchers, thieves, haters, liars, and worse, that is really good news. All you have to do is believe: Just say to him, "Jesus, I believe in you. Please come into my heart and clean me up. I want to be in your kingdom with you forever!"

---

4. New Living Translation.

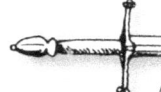
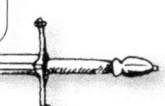

We should be thankful because we have a kingdom that cannot be shaken. And because we are thankful, we should worship God in a way that will please him. (**Hebrews 12:28**)

Have you ever heard the prayer that says, "Thy Kingdom come"? God's kingdom has already partly come, because wherever God is, there is his kingdom. But we don't live in it fully yet. When we die, we will go to live with him in his kingdom forever.

There will be a time when Jesus will come again to bring God's kingdom in its fullness. But right now, the world is still subject to the negative influences of the evil one, which we must learn to resist in that Great Battle. We'll talk more about that next.

Some questions for you:

1. In your own words, describe the kingdom of God.

2. Why did God go to the trouble of making a way for us to be with him in his kingdom despite our sinfulness?

3. Do you believe Jesus came to take the punishment for your sins and give you eternal life?

Notes:

9 • The Victorious Warrior

Now that you know about the spiritual world, let's get back to that Great Battle. You may ask, Who is fighting in this battle? The spiritual enemy of God, the father of lies, is fighting against God. This enemy of God is the very same one who showed up as a snake to convince Adam and Eve to believe his lies.

The enemy is working overtime all the time. Remember, he hates God—so he hates what God loves, which is you, the pinnacle of his creation. The enemy is busy trying to bring you down and lure you toward that which is destructive. Smoking pot, dipping into your parents' whiskey, playing with the occult, or visiting inappropriate websites may seem like no big thing at first, but they introduce a spiritual virus into your life that can spread and eventually destroy all that is good. The enemy would love nothing more than to do to you what he did to Adam and Eve—to convince you that you are your own god and can make up your own rules. But don't fall for that. He only wants to destroy you.

Like It or Not

You may say to yourself, "I don't want to be a part of this battle." You may wish that it were far away from you, but—like it or not—it is very near and very present. You can't escape it by ignoring it. In fact, you are at the heart of

> # The Bible tells us what the end will be. And it's good.

this battle, because you are the prize. Both sides want to win you. One side wants to win you so it can destroy you. The other side wants to win you so you can live your best life and dwell in freedom and joy in God's kingdom with him forever. Which side will be victorious in your life?

There is interplay between the spiritual world and the physical world. How does the spiritual battle show itself in the world around you? Whenever you see chaos, ugliness, filth, hate, destruction, lies, despair, and death, these are products of evil's influence. You can see these all around you in the world today.

On the other hand, order, cleanliness, love, building up, truth, joy, beauty, generosity, friendliness, and life are products of the influence of good. You can see these all around you in the world today also. These signs of good and evil show that even though the battle is invisible, it touches people's lives in very visible ways.

Even though evil might seem to gain ground, the good news is that in the end, good gets the victory over evil. We know this because the Bible tells us what the end will be. And it's good. But until then, the fight must go on. More than anything else, seek first God's kingdom and his righteousness, knowing that everything you need will be provided for you.

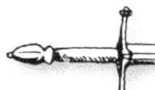

> *What you should want most is God's kingdom and doing what he wants you to do. Then he will give you all these other things you need.* (Matthew 6:33)

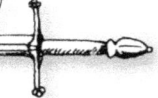

The Victorious Warrior

You are not alone in this battle. There is one who will always be by your side. The Victorious Warrior fights alongside you. Who is the Victorious Warrior? It is Jesus. Jesus can be known in many ways. He is pictured in the Bible as a captain of the Lord's armies with sword drawn. He is pictured as a lion and sometimes even as a sacrificial lamb. He is pictured as the one whose enemies will be a footstool for his feet.

Let's learn more about Jesus as the Victorious Warrior. Here is one description of him, where we see him "in your midst," which means he is right there with you. We also read that "he will rejoice over you with joy," which means you make this Victorious Warrior doubly happy—rejoicing with joy!

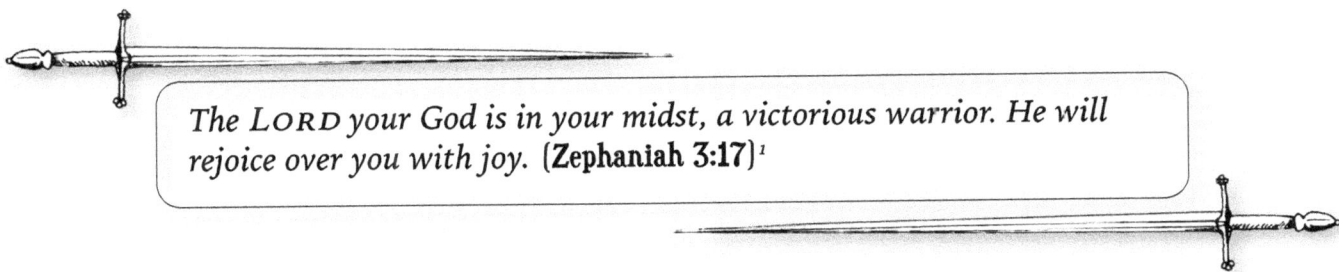

The LORD your God is in your midst, a victorious warrior. He will rejoice over you with joy. (**Zephaniah 3:17**)[1]

How is Jesus a warrior? In the spiritual world, Jesus achieved a very important victory in the Great Battle when he gave his life to take the punishment for our sins. We may wonder how that could be a victory. Didn't he die a painful death after being humiliated in front of the leaders and the people of his time? Though it looked like defeat for Jesus, in the spiritual realm, the cross was the resounding victory of the Victorious Warrior over God's enemy. He won a victory over sin and death.

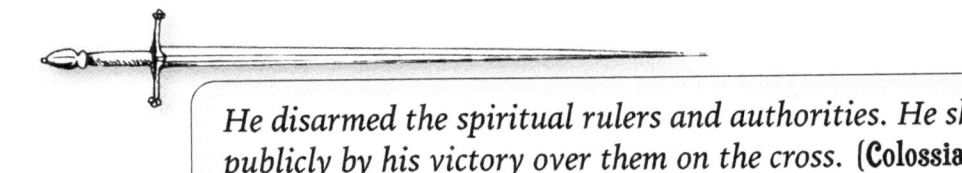

He disarmed the spiritual rulers and authorities. He shamed them publicly by his victory over them on the cross. (**Colossians 2:15**)[2]

---

1. New American Standard Bible.

2. New Living Translation.

His death on the cross is not the end of the story of what happened to Jesus. Though he died, he rose from the dead. He walked out of his tomb and won the final victory over death. This victory was also for us, because now we too have victory over death. When this life is over, we enter a new life that never ends. We are citizens in his kingdom forever. This takes away the sting of death and replaces it with a sweet hope of togetherness with God that will last for eternity.

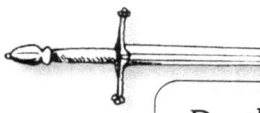

Death is swallowed up in victory. O death, where is your victory? O death, where is your sting? (**1 Corinthians 15:54-55**)[3]

The one who believes in Jesus enters into the everlasting victory that Jesus has already won and becomes a warrior in his victorious army. You are assured victory by standing under his battle banner. The Great Battle ends with the evil one being thrown into a lake of fire, never to be heard of again.

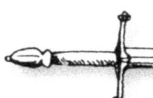

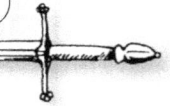

And the devil who deceived them was thrown into the lake of fire.... *The Son of God appeared for this purpose, to destroy the works of the devil.* (**Revelation 20:10**)[4]

Your Spiritual Warrior's Manual

Your prime instruction manual as a spiritual warrior is the Holy Bible. It is the ultimate guide for your spiritual life. The Bible is the story of God's

3. New Living Translation.

4. New American Standard Bible.

involvement in the lives of his beloved human creation over many thousands of years. It tells of people who loved and sought after God, and it tells of some who disobeyed him. It tells of the Victorious Warrior in all the facets of his character. It tells of his victories, frequently returning to the theme of his purpose that can never be defeated—that of saving humanity from sin.

The Bible is so many things. It is a book of history, poetry, and predictions of the future. It is also a love story. In a way, it tells of God's love for you. When you read it, you may discover the nearness of God as his truth is revealed to you. Amazingly, it is a living book, meaning that when you read it, God's words can work together with God's Holy Spirit living inside you such that you receive personal insights just for you.

Reading your Bible and thinking and praying about what you've read is a way to apply God's spiritual principles to your life. Make a habit of reading it regularly. Find adults who can help you with things in the Bible you don't understand. You may even wish to join a youth group at a church near you so you can study the Bible with others your age.

> *How can a young person live a clean life?*
> *By carefully reading the map of your [God's] Word.*
> *I'm single-minded in pursuit of you;*
> *don't let me miss the road signs you've posted.*
> *I've banked your promises in the vault of my heart*
> *so I won't sin myself bankrupt.* (**Psalm 119:9-11**)[5]

Your Spiritual Armor for the Battle

The Bible speaks of spiritual armor with which Jesus, the Victorious Warrior, equips you for the Great Battle. This armor is perfectly suited to spiritual warfare. He gives you the spiritual weapons to come out victorious and standing strong:

5. The Message Bible.

Wear the full armor of God. Wear God's armor so that you can fight against the devil's clever tricks. Our fight is not against people on earth. We are fighting against the rulers and authorities and the powers of this world's darkness. We are fighting against the spiritual powers of evil in the heavenly places. That is why you need to get God's full armor. Then on the day of evil, you will be able to stand strong. And when you have finished the whole fight, you will still be standing. **(Ephesians 6:11-13)**

According to the Bible, the pieces of your armor are:

• The belt of truth to wear under your armor. Jesus is the truth, so when you put on his truth first, you have the best foundation for the rest of your armor.

• The breastplate of righteousness. Jesus gives you his righteousness to cover you and protect your heart from evil.

• The sandals of the preparation of the Gospel of peace. You put these sandals on to step out and declare the goodness of Jesus.

• The shield of faith. This shield puts out the fiery darts the enemy shoots at you. His lies can't penetrate your faith in Jesus.

• The helmet of salvation. The salvation you received from Jesus when you believed in him protects your mind and ears from the attacks of the evil one like a helmet protects the head.

- The sword of the Spirit, which is the word of God. You have the word of God—your Bible. God's word is a mighty, sharp sword that cuts between truth and lies.[6]

But you have one more important weapon in the Great Battle, and that weapon is prayer.

Pray in the Spirit at all times. Pray with all kinds of prayers, and ask for everything you need. To do this you must always be ready. Never give up. (Ephesians 6:18)

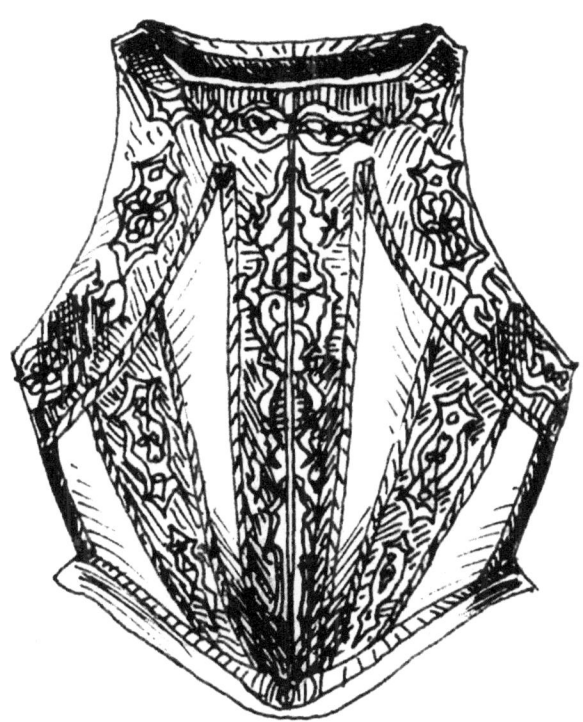

You may rely on the weapon of prayer every single day—many times a day, in fact. This is the communication channel where you can pour out your heart to God and he will hear you. Ask for the

6. Ephesians 6:14–17. This piece of armor is the inspiration behind the swords you see around the words from the Bible in this book.

Prayer is the communication channel where you can pour out your heart to God and he will hear you.

things you need, confess to him when you've done wrong along the way, and ask his forgiveness. Give thanks for the good things you've received and express your love and appreciation for God. These are all ways of praying.

Your spiritual armor is available to you all the time. You can imagine yourself putting it on as a way of preparing for the daily challenges of life. Then go with confidence that the Victorious Warrior walks beside you.

Some questions for you:

1. Do you ever sense that a spiritual battle is raging around you?

2. Do you have a church group that you can join to learn more about Jesus and the spiritual battle?

3. Do you have a Bible? If not, would you like one? If so, contact us at Bibles@VictoriousWarrior.org and we will send you one for free.

4. What is something in your life that makes you rejoice with joy, like the Victorious Warrior rejoices over you?

Notes:

10 • Who's Gonna Be the Boss?

The challenges of a spiritual warrior are not trivial. You will be tested. Your first duty is to be prepared for battle. One way that the Holy Spirit works in you is to help you exercise self-control. Self-control is one of what we call the "fruits of the Spirit."[1] For you to be equal to the challenges you will face in life, you must learn to restrain your desires, and—in short—*be the boss*. This is one of the hardest and most important things to learn in developing a spiritual warrior's mindset and, in the long run, the most rewarding.

Controlling Your Desires

Who's going to be the boss? Who's the one that's going to be in control of your choices? Is it going to be your better judgment? Or are your desires going to control you? Do you remember Mr. Feel-Likit and Ms. Don-Wanna? They do what they want right now without thinking of tomorrow. Miss Ought-to and Mr. Do-Right have long-term goals that take them beyond feeding their immediate desires.

An example of this may be when you choose to spend your afternoon studying for an upcoming test instead of playing with your VR headset. When you exercise in preparation for the big game instead of staying glued to the

---

1. All the fruits of the Spirit are found at Galatians 5:22–23.

couch watching YouTube. When you save your money instead of throwing it away on every little treat that comes across your path. When you keep your dinner portion size reasonable and chew your food instead of stuffing your face like a ravenous wolf.

Let's be specific about what is meant by your desires. Certainly, if you're hungry, it is not unhealthy to desire to eat. But some desires are unhealthy and unrelated to real needs. They lead you down a path that is not good for you. So, being the boss of your desires means that you gratify your desires within the

> **Being the boss of your desires means that you gratify your desires within the limits of what is healthy and what keeps you aiming toward the good.**

limits of what is healthy and what keeps you aiming toward the good. You do not let gratifying your desires spill over into self-indulgence and behaviors that cause harm to yourself or others.

Some of the most common challenges to being the boss of your desires are in the areas of social media, sexual thoughts and behaviors, and mind-altering drugs and alcohol. Many have fallen at the hands of the enemy in the Great Battle because of weakness in one or more of these areas. Each of them can be addictive, which makes them all the more dangerous when you misuse

them. Addiction means that you are always hungry for more. It causes your desires to gnaw at you, scream at you, and pester you to feed them, but they are never filled—and guess what? No matter how much you feed them, they never even say thank you.

The evil one tries to mimic God by offering things that seem similar to the good things God has for you, but the enemy's things do harm instead of good. In the area of social media, the enemy offers phantom online "friends" in place of true friendship. In the area of physical intimacy, the enemy offers lust in place of true love. In the area of mind-altering drugs and alcohol, the enemy offers the happiness of a temporary high instead of the true joy that God offers.

Remember that the evil one wants to destroy the things God loves. He asks himself, "How can I wound God most?" The answer is by destroying those made in his image—that is, you. Today we find that young people—people your age and even younger—are targeted more and more by the evil one. In the face of these temptations, can you triumph? Of course, by putting on your spiritual armor, relying on your warrior's handbook, the Bible, and standing with Jesus, the Victorious Warrior, the answer is yes.

Building Muscle Memory

When you were a baby, you were that fluffy bundle of insistent demands wrapped up in an adorable package. But you're not a baby anymore. Being able to resist the insistent demands of your desires is what it means to mature. It's never easy, but like anything else, practice strengthens you. It's never too late to start developing the habit of *restraining your desires*.

Restrain: To hold back; to check; to hold from action, proceeding or advancing, either by physical or moral force.

Every day of your life, with every choice you make, you are creating habits—building muscle memory—doing things over and over and getting good at them. If you practice difficult things, in time they become easier for you. If you put your mind to practicing rowing or piano or writing computer programs, you improve those skills. If you practice the art of listening to others when they are speaking to you—which is extremely difficult, by the way—you get better at it.

On the other hand, if you "practice" harmful things, you get pretty "good" at them too, and they impact you negatively by becoming habitual and, in time, degrading you. You must practice a daily habit of self-restraint to be the boss of your desires. Put aside some quiet time to reflect on how you handle the things that happen to you from day to day and how you can do better tomorrow. When you are challenged, that is a great opportunity to use that powerful weapon of prayer and ask the Victorious Warrior, Jesus, to help you.

In the next three chapters, we're going to focus on those three areas we mentioned—social media, sex, and drugs and alcohol—and talk about ways to be the boss of your desires in those areas.

Be confident that with God's help and your warrior's mindset, you can be victorious over even the most difficult challenges.

Some questions for you:

1. Talk about a time when you were the boss of your desires.

2. Have you ever experienced how practicing something makes you better at it?

3. Did you ever notice how easy it is to misuse things that are meant to be good for you?

Notes:

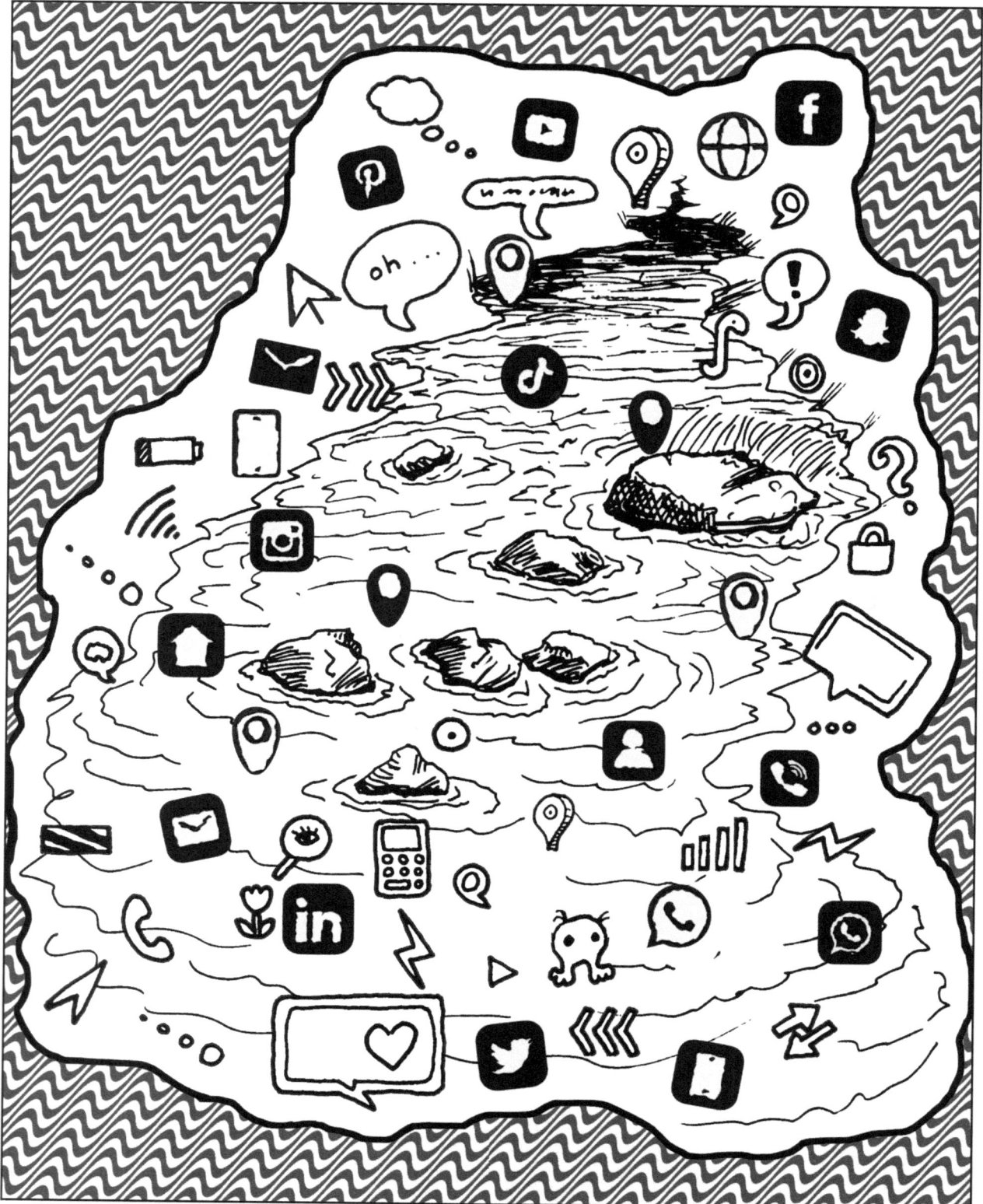

11 • The Raging River

Wow. The internet is crazy. Last night, I sat down with my device and came across a video of racing hamsters wearing Formula One race-car costumes. Then, as I scrolled, I saw where a guy was having his brain scanned and discovered he had a twin inside his head. Really? Then some deep-sea divers were pulling aliens out of a sunken submarine. Then a toilet was singing "Here Comes Santa Claus." Then a puppet made out of a real fish. Then unicorn stew. Then skeletons. Then squishy. Then, then, then, then…

That's when I realized I was doomscrolling, and hours had slipped away from me—never to be seen again. I felt like I had been swooshed down a raging river to a place far, far away, and my feet couldn't find any solid ground to stand on. I had just given away precious hours of my life, and I had nothing to show for them. That internet river was trying to drown me, and it almost succeeded.

Sometimes it seems like the whole world has turned into a raging river of pictures flickering across our devices. We can't keep our eyes off the cascade of shiny lights. Each post is the most important thing in the world for a microsecond, and then it's gone and something else is the most important thing in the world—for a microsecond. So nothing is important in any lasting way, and we begin to crave anything just because it's new. In the end, we're left empty and sitting alone with our devices in front of our faces, craving the next new thing. And meanwhile, life rushes away down the rapids.

Do you live in the crazy, raging social-media river? It could be YouTube or video games or VR or social media or any other raging river of meaningless noise. Do you ever feel that there's no solid ground to stand on? Does it ever make your life feel empty? Do you ever wonder if there's more to your life than snapchats and likes and reels and tik-toks and tumbles?

> **Whatever truth there is to be found in the raging river is swimming in a soup of lies that some influencer said on some platform somewhere.**

The raging river doesn't know good from bad or right from wrong. It doesn't know you or care about you. It only cares that it keeps you engaged for another few seconds. The next thing you know, hours have passed and you have to go through a reality-re-entry process like an astronaut returning from outer space. These mindless activities can be a place where the enemy will entice you to throw away your life.

Noisy Lies

The noise of that raging river can drown out the voice of your God-given moral compass—this is one of its dangers. To hear the sound of God's guiding voice, you have to quiet all the distractions, take a moment, and listen.

You might think you're going to find answers to the big questions about life in that raging river. But whatever truth there is to be found in the raging river is swimming in a soup of lies that some influencer said on some platform somewhere. It's hard to tell truth from lies.

One example of lies taking over social media is the lie that you may have been born in the wrong body and your gender is based on your feelings rather than the facts of your chromosomes. Teens suffering confusion about who they are as they go through puberty are perfect targets for those pushing this ridiculous notion. The solution being sold on social media is for boys to cut

off their perfectly good boy parts and "become girls" and for girls to cut off their perfectly healthy girl parts and "become boys."

This is a perfect example of the Great Battle and how the enemy is trying to destroy you. All young people naturally go through a temporary awkward stage as you grow in your teen years, and surgically and chemically damaging your body to pretend you're something you're not *only makes things worse.* That is not how you follow your code to love truth.

In time, as you mature, you will naturally grow out of those awkward feelings about your body and accept who you are. Everyone goes through it. And just because you're a tomboy-type girl, or you're a boy who is gentle by nature, or you may feel some attraction to the same sex does not mean you're gay or trans. In a little while, you'll see things differently. You're growing and changing constantly, and your hormones at your age are coursing through your body, affecting your feelings. So take a deep breath and relax.

More and more trans people are coming forward, speaking about their regret that they fell for that lie. They are telling the tragic truth about their grief, their lifelong health problems from taking hormones and getting surgery to change their bodies, and their longing for things they can't get back. Some are suing the irresponsible doctors and therapists that manipulated them into making such calamitous decisions. Many of them wonder why some grown-up didn't step forward and warn them. That's one reason we're speaking to you about it now.

There's no turning back after making the choice to transition. Boys and girls are left permanently scarred, under doctors' care, and dependent on pharmaceuticals, without ever having experienced what it means to be a grown man or woman in their natural body. Don't fall for this lie of the enemy.

Today, research shows that the majority of those who transition were persuaded to do so online through social media, blogs, and YouTube…. The chemical and surgical interventions used for gender transition cause health problems like cardiovascular disease, reduced bone density, and, ultimately, sterilization. They don't even improve mental health in the long run: Those who surgically transition are 19 times more likely to commit suicide than their peers.[1]

More and More Lies

Another danger found in the raging river is that people sometimes are not who they say they are. Maybe you've heard tales of young girls being drawn into relationships on social media only to discover that their "fifteen-year-old boyfriend" turns out to be a fifty-year-old lecher who wants to lure them away from the safety of home. Always have your antennae up looking for clues to identify those with bad intentions. Forewarned is forearmed in this battle.

Healthy relationships are more apt to be found in person, face to face, where you can see the person you're getting to know. You can assess their

---

1. Jared Eckert and Mary McClosky, "How Big Tech Turns Kids Trans," The Heritage Foundation, September 15, 2022, heritage.org/gender/commentary/how-big-tech-turns-kids-trans; "In the study, people with gender dysphoria who had ever used hormone replacements saw nearly seven times the risk of ischemic stroke (a blockage in a vessel supplying blood to the brain), nearly six times the risk of ST elevation myocardial infarction (the most serious type of heart attack) and nearly five times the risk of pulmonary embolism (a blockage in an artery in the lung), compared with people with gender dysphoria who had never used hormone replacements." Katie Glenn, "Hormone Therapy for Gender Dysphoria May Raise Cardiovascular Risks," American College of Cardiology, Feb 23, 2023, acc.org/About-ACC/Press-Releases/2023/02/22/20/29/Hormone-Therapy-for-Gender-Dysphoria-May-Raise-Cardiovascular-Risks.

> The reason addiction is a particular problem for teens is that your brains are still developing and are easily entrapped by addiction—much more easily than grown-ups.

character—whether they're dangerous or trustworthy. You can read their body language. You can hang out and get burgers, go for a walk, and meet their family.

Yet another danger is that as you consume more and more social media, you can become addicted to that raging river. The reason addiction is a particular problem for teens is that your brains are still developing and are easily entrapped by addiction—much more easily than grown-ups. Also, it's harder to break addictions that are started when you're young. Addiction in one area will lead to addiction in other areas.

Did you know that many tech moguls don't even allow their own children on social media?[2] This is because they know its dangers. Maybe the wise choice is to follow their lead.

So, we ask, who's going to be the boss when it comes to social media? Spiritual warriors work to be the masters of their desires. To be in control of your desires is to take your place as the boss. What are some good choices you can make regarding social media?

• Put the device down.

• Make physical activity a priority.

• Notice how you feel after spending time on social media. Does it make you depressed? Self-critical? Envious of others? Don't let the enemy use social media to define your identity. God's love for you is the source of your identity.

---

2. Katie A. Paul, "Tech Execs Protect Their Kids from Their Own Products. America's Children Deserve the Same," *Fast Company*, May 24, 2023, fastcompany.com/90900166/tech-social-media=protection-children.

- Set limits on the time you spend on social media.

- Make sharp distinctions between necessary use of your devices and the raging river.

- Keep your devices in a public area of your home so you will not be tempted to go to bad websites.

- Find activities to take the place of the raging river, such as nature walks, crafts, juggling, poetry, learning a language, sports, or games.

- Consider walking away from social media altogether.

- Find a real book. Hold it in your hands. Open it. Smell it. Read it.

- Turn off some of your notifications.

- Make friends with real people.

- Pick up your Bible and read it. It's full of truth, not lies.

There is a life for you outside the raging river, and the more you step out of the noise, the more you will learn to value real life. That's part of what loving truth is all about—knowing the difference between flashing lights on a screen and reality.

Your life is precious, has purpose, and should not be wasted. You'll be surprised how good it will make you feel to spend some reality time. Here, let me help you out of that river. Take my hand. Here's a towel.

Some questions for you:

1. How can the love of truth as found in your code help you to be the boss in the area of social media?

2. How can the pursuit of excellence as found in your code help you to be the boss in the area of social media?

3. How can service to others as found in your code help you to be the boss in the area of social media?

Notes:

12 • Getting Personal

Now for the difficult subject of sex. It is a very personal subject, yet people talk about it a lot. But when people talk about sex, they usually don't include the most important part: what God intended for it. We need to talk about it because if you learn about sex from the internet or other unreliable sources, you will get a distorted view. We need to talk about it because if you're a spiritual warrior committed to aiming toward the good, this is one area where it *really matters* that you are the boss of your desires.

What Is Sex?

What is sex, anyway? You may have noticed that all around you, the world is full of creatures, and there's a never-ending supply of them. This is by God's design. He wants to fill the earth with an abundance of his creation. He does this by giving males and females an attraction to one another. God made sex pleasurable so that animals and humans would procreate and enjoy being together in closeness.

In the case of humans, this closeness takes on an even more important value—love. When two humans have sex, they bond together in love. A long-term relationship in which the man and woman are committed to each other makes it possible to raise children and work together as a team—that is, a family.

 God intended for sex between a man and a woman to take place only within the context of a committed marriage. The Bible makes this clear, and research confirms that the brain-mapping process that binds two together during sex changes with every additional sex partner. When people have lots of partners, they are less and less able to form long-term, bonded relationships.

Besides making more humans, sex is God's way for a husband and wife to grow closer in their special marriage relationship. It is a way for them to show love to each other and bring delight, joy, and satisfaction to one another. During times of physical intimacy, the husband and wife build trust, intimacy, gentle playfulness, and caring. Their physical union is a treasure to share just between the two of them.

Physical intimacy between man and woman is also the way babies are made, turning husbands into fathers, wives into mothers, and two into a family. As a father, the husband grows as a man by protecting, providing for, and guiding his family. As a mother, the wife grows as a woman by building a home, nurturing young ones, and transmitting meaning to the next generation. These are extremely important tasks, as healthy families are the foundation of a healthy society.[1] You can see that sex in its proper place affects the whole world.

Trampling on the Sacred

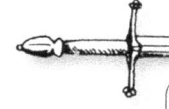

> *Can you carry fire against your chest without burning your clothes?*
> *(Proverbs 6:27)*[2]

Sex is not something to be played with. It is like fire. In the fireplace (in a loving marriage), fire is a good thing. It warms the house. But when that

---

1. Not everyone becomes a parent, and those who do not are no less valuable. But even those who don't become parents find ways to show their intrinsic mothering and fathering natures—for example, as beloved uncles and aunts, pet lovers, teachers, coaches, and mentors.

2. Good News Translation.

> # For God, the union between a husband and wife is sacred.

fire spills out of the fireplace (outside of marriage and with multiple partners), it becomes dangerous. The whole house can burn down.

For God, the union between a husband and wife is sacred. It is meant to symbolize the special, intimate relationship between Jesus and those who believe in him. God even pictures the great day when his kingdom fully comes as a wedding banquet. Jesus Christ is the groom, and believers who follow Jesus Christ (male and female alike) are considered his bride.

Therefore, any kind of sex that doesn't fit into that sacred picture of the marriage between Jesus and his bride (Jesus followers) is a twisting of God's purposes for sex. Then, what God meant for good becomes damaging. When sex occurs outside of the protective marriage framework God designed for it, it is cheapened. It is like taking a bowl made of purest gold and using it as a chamber pot.[3] Sex is cheapened further by skipping from one partner to another, with no lasting, meaningful connection to any one partner.

Other examples of twisting God's purposes for sex include looking at inappropriate pictures and videos and pleasuring oneself. Both can be extremely addictive. They create distorted, unreal expectations of how sex looks and what it is for.

When practiced outside of God's design for sex, before you know it, this sacred gift is reduced to a hollow, meaningless act. Not far down this path we find broken relationships, divorce, betrayal, disappointment, low self-worth, and shame. This is not the path to healthy,

> **Sacred:** Holy; pertaining to God or to his worship; separated from common secular uses and consecrated to God and his service.

---

3. In the old days before flush toilets, people used chamber pots (pots in your bed chamber) as toilets.

one-on-one relationships that lead to marriage and family building. Just as healthy families mean a healthy society, the breakdown of the family leads to more crime, children without fathers, sexually transmitted diseases, addiction, mental illness, and other social problems. These ills are signs of the evil one gaining ground in the Great Battle. God's enemy takes what is sacred to God and perverts it.

Letting your hungers be the boss in the area of sex causes you to live in the darkness of secrecy and hidden sin. You end up feeling like you're living a lie, as you may look good on the outside, but inside you are in the grip of shame.

Another of the casualties of sex outside of marriage is that the babies that come along from those ungodly unions are often destroyed through abortion. This not only takes the life of a developing human being with a beating heart, but it is a trauma that can leave lifelong scars on the mom and dad who make that awful choice.

Filling an Emptiness

Sometimes people get physically intimate because they are longing to make connections that will fill them up and relieve their loneliness. But there are so many wonderful, healthy ways to connect with others aside from sex, and the other ways don't have all the dangers that come with getting physical. True companionship and friendship can heal loneliness in a way that sex can't. Some get physically intimate because being sexually desired makes them feel they have value. But our true value is found in the love God has for us, not in the fleeting, momentary desires of others.

> Our true value is found in the love God has for us, not in the fleeting, momentary desires of others.

You will also find that growing your relationship with Jesus by studying the Bible, preferably in a church home with people your age who love Jesus, can heal loneliness in a way that nothing else can.

So, who's going to be the boss of your sexuality? Again, it's all about control of your desires. Your sexual urges are part of who you are and part of being attractive and attracted to others. Your desire to be with a love partner is natural. But it is important for you to wait to get the best of what God has for you in his design for sex within marriage.

What can you do to be the boss in the area of your sexual desires?

- Set clear boundaries, stick to them, and make sure your boy- or girlfriend knows your boundaries and respects them.

- Stay away from situations that might trigger you or weaken you, such as parties, taking drugs, drinking, or being alone with someone of the opposite sex.

- Keep your phone charger in a public part of your home, and **NEVER** take your phone to bed with you at night.

- Don't let anyone ever pressure or bully you into doing things you ought not to do. Seek help if you are being pressured or bullied. This is not okay.

- Is there someone you trust that you can talk to? It helps to be accountable to someone you can trust.

- Pour out your heart to Jesus. He is always ready to listen to you, and he knows what you're going through.

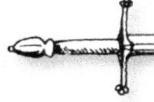

> *And now he [Jesus] can help those who are tempted. He is able to help because he himself suffered and was tempted.* (Hebrew 2:18)

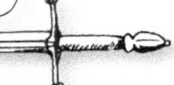

Some questions for you:

1. How can the love of truth as found in your code help you to be the boss in the area of physical intimacy?

2. How can the pursuit of excellence as found in your code help you to be the boss in the area of physical intimacy?

3. How can service to others as found in your code help you to be the boss in the area of physical intimacy?

Notes:

13 • Mind Altering

The last of our challenging subjects is drugs and alcohol. Drugs and alcohol to humans act something like an enticing worm does to a fish. They offer an alluring promise of pleasure, but beware—like the worm, that pleasure has a hook in it. Don't be the foolish fish that gets caught on that hook.

You may see people who seem to be having fun getting drunk and high and living the party life. But look at where that leads. Drugs and alcohol change your brain in a way that makes quitting very hard and leads to addictive dependence. When you are addicted, all you care about is getting more drugs or alcohol into your system, and soon, nothing else matters. This is where the enemy wins the battle by separating you from reality and from useful pursuits. Your life becomes focused on just getting high. Take a look at many city streets and see the wasted people slumped in corners or roaming around looking for their next hit. It is a dead end, and it is very sad. This is not the picture of a warrior in the army of the Victorious Warrior, Jesus.

Is It Worth the Risk?

When you use drugs and alcohol, you take risks in many areas of your life. Let's start with school. Many of those who start taking drugs as young people lose motivation to excel in school. Studies show that students who get high get worse grades.[1] Drugs destroy the parts of the brain that should be expanding and learning at your age. The human brain doesn't stop developing until you reach age twenty-five or so. You have a lot of important growing to do now.

People who drink and use drugs also risk damaging their physical health. They might contract HIV, hepatitis, heart disease, cancer, stroke, and sexually transmitted diseases. Their immune systems suffer, making them vulnerable to other illnesses.

They even risk death.

> *Fentanyl—which is about 50 times stronger than heroin—is almost entirely responsible for a spike in youth overdose deaths in California, where such incidents were once rarer than in the rest of the country.... Some young people buy pills from dealers over social media thinking they're pure oxycodone, Xanax or Adderall, but they're increasingly laced with fentanyl. Others knowingly ingest the drug, a risk when just 2 milligrams can end a person's life.[2]*

If you think you're safe "just smoking pot," don't be fooled. Pot can do plenty of damage. And beware that drug dealers are now putting fentanyl and other extremely powerful and deadly substances in marijuana to increase the high. One hit could mean the end for you. *There is no safe drug!*

There is no safe drug!

You also risk damaging your mental health. Here is a list of possible effects on your mental health from drug and alcohol use:

- Needing to take more to get the same effect
- Feeling like you must use the drug or alcohol
- Withdrawal symptoms when you don't use, including feeling sick, cold, sweaty, or shaky

1. "Making the Connection: Drug Use and Academic Grades," U.S. Department of Health and Human Services, cdc.gov/healthyyouth/health_and_academics/pdf/DASHFactSheetDrugUse.pdf.

2. Blake Jones, "Teen Overdose Deaths Lead California Schools to Stock Reversal drug," *Politico*, February 5, 2023, politico.com/news/2023/02/05/teen-overdose-deaths-california-schools-narcan-00081186.

- Sudden mood changes
- A negative outlook on life
- Anxiety
- Being secretive and deceptive to cover up what you're doing
- Drug-induced psychosis[3]

You might even risk having thoughts of suicide.

Using drugs and alcohol can cause your whole life to spin out of control because when you are high, you are more likely to use poor judgment and do things you will regret later, such as getting physically intimate, drunken fights, and getting DUIs,[4] for example. When you come down off that high, you may also have a giant mess to clean up involving friends, family, or the law.

> When you come down off that high, many times you've got a giant personal mess to clean up.

People who live like this also age quickly, becoming dull-witted, unproductive, and smelly. Trouble follows them wherever they go. They have a hard time reaching goals because they've spent all their energy running after phantoms. And in their quiet moments of solitude, they are left hung over, depressed, lost, lonely, and searching for meaning. They find that their friends aren't very dependable and don't have their interests in mind because they've gone looking for their own high.

---

3. "Drugs, Alcohol & Mental Health," Rethink Mental Illness, accessed February 9, 2023, rethink.org/advice-and-information/about-mental-illness/learn-more-about-conditions/drugs-alcohol-and-mental-health/.

4. DUI means "driving under the influence" of alcohol or drugs.

Some people get drunk or high to get away from their problems. They go up onto the mountaintop, and then they come down the mountain, and guess what? Their problems are still sitting there waiting for them. These activities are not those of a spiritual warrior.

Don't Start

How can you avoid becoming hooked on drugs and alcohol? The best way is to not start to begin with. When your friends are urging you to join them, maybe it's time to find a new set of friends. Here are some ideas to help you, a spiritual warrior, avoid the evil one's trap of drugs and alcohol. How can you be the boss in this area?

- Surround yourself with healthy friends who don't do drugs and alcohol and who are going somewhere in life.

- Get involved in healthy activities like sports, hobbies, classes you love, learning new things, and being outdoors.

- Learn to cope with your difficult feelings. Everyone has them. Burying them won't make them go away. Talk to someone you trust, find a mentor, keep a journal, or speak to a counselor. Often, these difficult feelings will just pass in time.

- Don't allow yourself to be pressured into doing things that are not good for you. Be your own person.

- Establish a daily prayer life so you can hear God's voice guiding you through the difficult moments of life. Seek his wisdom for you through reading the Bible, and call out to him in your moments of weakness. He will hear you.

- Here is a Bible verse for you to think and pray about:

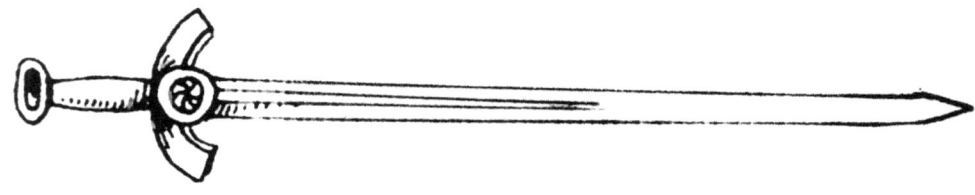

"I am allowed to do anything," you say. My answer to this is that not all things are good. Even if it is true that "I am allowed to do anything," I will not let anything control me like a slave.
(1 Corinthians 6:12)

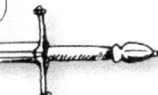

Some questions for you:

1. How can the love of truth as found in your code help you to be the boss in the area of drugs and alcohol?

2. How can the pursuit of excellence as found in your code help you to be the boss in the area of drugs and alcohol?

3. How can service to others as found in your code help you to be the boss in the area of drugs and alcohol?

Notes:

14 • So, Are You Going to Be the Boss?

Oscar's food truck is just down the road. Maybe I should have taken a hint when I heard someone call it the "Roach Coach." Anyway, my curiosity got the better of me, and now I'm here to warn you with my tale of woe: I ate at Oscar's last night, and when I got home, I nearly puked my guts out. I was hovering over the toilet all night long, trembling in cold sweats, like flaming dragons were eating their way out of my belly. Whatever you do, *DO NOT* eat at Oscar's!

Okay, so that's my tale. Now that you've heard it, what about you? Are you going to go eat at Oscar's? Maybe you are the type of person who needs to find out for yourself. You might insist, "But I hear Oscar's food is cheap and the portions are huge!"

Or, after hearing my tale, you may growl, "Nobody tells me what to do! I'll eat whatever I want, wherever I want. In fact, just because you told me not to, I'm heading over to Oscar's right now!"

But just maybe, instead you will say, "I can learn from that person's experience, especially when it could end up really bad for me." You will choose to stay as far away from Oscar's as you can, thus saving yourself that big bellyache.

A Smart Person and a Wise Person

This is the difference between a *smart person* and a *wise person*: A smart person may make bad choices, but he learns from his mistakes and doesn't repeat them. That's great—you should learn from your bad choices.

But even better than a smart person is the one who learns from *other people's* bad choices. This is what is called a wise person. A wise person will look at other people's bad choices and see the consequences. This will allow that person to think before acting to make the better choice.

We won't even talk about foolish people—those who won't even learn from their own bad choices. Some will go to Oscar's Roach Coach and get that Tuesday 'Tomaine Special[1] again and again and again.

> You can spare yourself lots of trouble and heartache in the areas of social media, physical intimacy, and drugs and alcohol by heeding the warnings you've just read.

Be the Boss

Maybe a few of you reading this book will recognize the warnings presented here and will want to avoid making bad choices. Maybe you will be persuaded by the mistakes of others that it is wise to make choices for yourself that will lead to good outcomes. Some choices you make will have lifelong consequences, so pay attention! You can spare yourself lots of trouble and heartache in the areas of social media, physical intimacy, and drugs and alcohol by heeding the warnings you've just read. In other words, *DO NOT* eat at Oscar's!

---

1. *Ptomaine* is a very dangerous bacteria that makes you really, *really* sick.

We've looked at three particularly dangerous areas where addiction and unhealthy desire can challenge your warrior's mindset. Yet, there are many dangers we have not discussed here that are equally destructive. To name a few, there are witchcraft and the occult, hatred and unforgiveness, pride, envy, idolizing anything in place of God, and anger. According to the Bible, many of these wrong behaviors lead us toward death and destruction and away from the good:

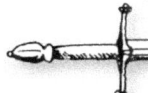

> *The wrong things the sinful self does are clear:*
>
> - committing sexual sin,
> - being morally bad,
> - doing all kinds of shameful things,
> - worshiping false gods,
> - taking part in witchcraft,
> - hating people,
> - causing trouble,
> - being jealous, angry or selfish,
> - causing people to argue and divide into separate groups,
> - being filled with envy,
> - getting drunk,
> - having wild parties,
>
> *and doing other things like this. I warn you now as I warned you before: The people who do these things will not have a part in God's kingdom. (Galatians 5:19-21)*

If your destination is the kingdom of God, these things will throw you off the path. In fact, they will take you in the opposite direction of where you

> **In order to be an effective warrior aiming toward the good, you need to have your body healthy, your mind clear, and your spirit tuned to Jesus.**

want to end up, which is exactly where the enemy of God wants you to be. They're like heading to the North Pole by way of Antarctica.

In order to be an effective warrior aiming toward the good, you need to have your body healthy, your mind clear, and your spirit tuned to Jesus. This is how you will be able to make good choices for the best outcomes. As you grow, you'll see that where you are in life is a result of the choices you have made along the way. Choosing to be boss over your desires means that you, not the desires, are going to be in control, regardless of how they may rise up in you. With Jesus's help, you can be victorious.

You are young, but don't let anyone treat you as if you are not important. Be an example to show the believers how they should live. Show them by what you say, by the way you live, by your love, by your faith, and by your pure life. (1 Timothy 4:12)

But what about when you fail? We'll answer that question in the next chapter.

Some questions for you:

1. Talk about a time you ignored a warning and paid the price for it.

2. Talk about a time you learned from watching the mistakes made by others.

3. Name one area of your life where you need to work on becoming the boss.

Notes:

15 • What About When You Fail?

With every step you take along the warrior's path, you move closer to your goal of becoming the warrior that the Victorious Warrior, Jesus, calls you to be. This is a lifelong process. Remember that practicing good habits helps you develop muscle memory so those habits become easier and easier to maintain. But sometimes the path gets lost amongst the brambles and boulders. In the Great Battle, the enemy will take any and every opportunity to try and trip you up.

So, what about when you stumble? If you do find that you have fallen off the warrior's path and given in to unhealthy desires, it is not too late to turn around. It's never too late, no matter how many times you stumble. Stop where you are, take stock, and know that you can get back on track no matter what.

It's so important to remember that there is only one perfect warrior, and that is the Victorious Warrior, Jesus. All of the rest of us miss the mark as we go through life. It's just part of being human. We all fall off the path at some time or another.

The Example of Jonah

Jonah in the Bible was one who fell off the path. God had an assignment for him, and instead of doing as God asked, Jonah ran in the other direction and tried to get as far away from God as he could so he wouldn't have to do what he was asked. But God wouldn't let Jonah off the hook. Jonah was trying to escape in a boat, so God sent a huge fish to swallow him up and take him to the very bottom of the sea. With that new perspective from the inside of a fish's gullet, Jonah found the following words. Notice his certainty that God will pull him out of an impossible situation he brought on himself:

> *I was in very bad trouble. I called to the Lord for help, and he answered me. I was deep in the grave. I cried to you, and you heard my voice.* (**Jonah 2:2**)

Okay, so you stumbled. You do not have permission to stay down. Get up and get back on the path. The sooner you make that turnaround, the sooner you will be in the boss's seat again.

Let Jesus Be Your Strength

Remember, you are not in this battle alone. You have the Victorious Warrior by your side. The first thing you must do when you stumble is call out to that Victorious Warrior, Jesus, and tell him, "Help! I'm stuck!" You can call out to Jesus:

> *Jesus, you see I'm in need of help. I let my unhealthy desires be my boss. Help me to be a victorious warrior like you. I am weak, and I rely on your strength for help. Please be my strength.*

Tell Jesus what you have done and ask his forgiveness. Ask him to help you turn around and get back on track. Jesus's victory does not leave you in your failure. He will pull you out of the depths like he did Jonah.

Your next step is to honestly examine yourself and look at the choices you made that led you to your situation so that you can learn from your mistake. Be willing to take responsibility for your part. Tell this to Jesus as well.

Whenever you ask for his forgiveness with a contrite heart, he will forgive you, even if you've already gotten many second chances. He wants to help you. Today is a new day. You have a friend in Jesus. His mercies are new every morning.

Contrite: Broken-hearted for sin; deeply affected with grief and sorrow for having offended God; humble.

But in all these things we overwhelmingly conquer through him who loved us. (**Romans 8:37**)

By relying on Jesus's strength to help you overcome your failings, you are holding him up as the source of your strength. His strength becomes a reason for you to boast about your weakness.

Every day is a new day in the Great Battle. You can daily renew your commitment to your code of conduct and your resolve to aim toward the good. You can daily don your spiritual armor and take up your sword, which is the Word of God. Yesterday's failures do not have to keep you down. Today, you may rise up and deal that evil one a mighty blow to the head. Remember, with the Victorious Warrior, the battle can be won.

To be aided in your daily life, consider joining forces with others who are on the same

> **Yesterday's failures do not have to keep you down. Today, you may rise up and deal that evil one a mighty blow to the head.**

warrior's path as you. Fellow warriors working together can be accountable to one another. You can help one another when one of you falls. You can spur each other on, offer compassion, and motivate each other. Find fellow warriors.

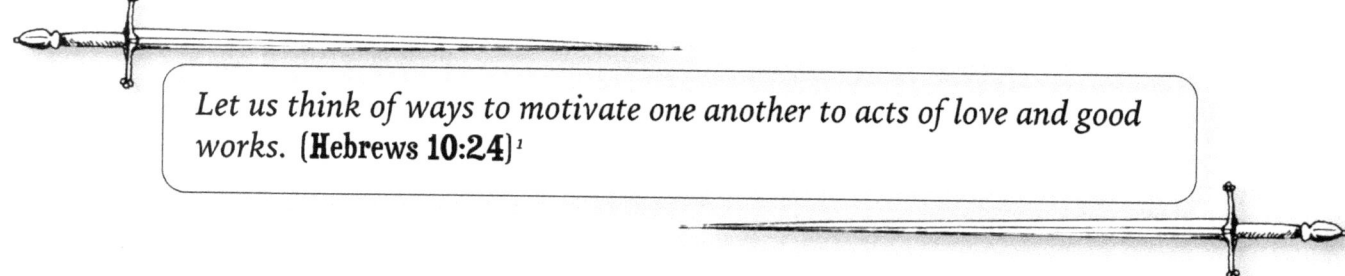

> *Let us think of ways to motivate one another to acts of love and good works.* (Hebrews 10:24)[1]

Finding a church that focuses on young people is a good way to join with others who are on the warrior's path.

Practical Steps

Let's review these steps you can take if you fall off the warrior's path:

- Call out to Jesus for help.
- Tell Jesus what you've done and ask him to forgive you.
- Examine yourself to learn from your mistake. Take responsibility for your part.
- Rely on Jesus's strength.
- Renew your commitment to your warrior's path.
- Join forces with other warriors like yourself.

---

1. New Living Translation.

Some questions for you:

1. How did being inside a fish's belly change Jonah's perspective?

2. When you stumble and fall, what can you do to get back on the warrior's path?

3. Talk about a time when you took responsibility for your mistakes.

Notes:

16 • The Rest of the Story

It's time to return to the story of the long-legged boy and the curly-haired girl. When we left them, they had just suffered a heartbreaking consequence of their poor choices and their me-centered life of doing as they pleased.

You might think that they learned from their mistake, but you would be wrong. They thought they could just go right back to living as they were used to, doing what they felt like doing according to their own rules, with no one telling them what to do. That's just what they tried to do.

As it happened, within mere months, the curly-haired girl had a new baby growing in her womb. As awful as that first experience was, they couldn't think of any other choice than to make yet another appointment at another one of those dark, gloomy offices to have this new baby removed. They had not learned their lesson.

Well, God was about to show himself to the long-legged boy and the curly-haired girl one more time in a new way.

Time Stops

At this appointment, the long-legged boy and curly-haired girl noticed a cluster of people praying quietly outside near the entrance. The curly-haired girl didn't understand what they were doing there. She went inside, paid her money, and sat down to wait. This time, she sat alone. Her thoughts turned inward. These words from her past came back to her memory:

There is One who watches over you and cares about you. He is the source of all that is good, and in your darkest hour of need, He will find you, make you His own, and give you a home where you belong. But be sure to resist the evil one, for he is the one that lives in shadows. You can find order if you love truth, if you do all things with excellence, and if you give yourself over to serve others.

> **God seemed to stop time and put a wall of protection around her so she could just sit and think about what she was doing.**

"Could I really find a home where I truly belong?" the curly-haired girl wondered. "Could I learn to serve others? Maybe I could start by learning to serve the child inside of me," she thought. Her resolve slowly grew as she thought and thought.

She didn't realize that a full hour had passed since her appointment time, yet somehow, no one came to fetch her to go into the private room at the back. God seemed to stop time and put a wall of protection around her so she could just sit and think about what she was doing.

It was then in that dreary little waiting room that the curly-haired girl decided, "I'm going to keep my child!"

Meanwhile, the long-legged boy was sitting in the van, waiting for her to come out. Something was happening inside him as well. Some long-buried words came to his remembrance:

God wore a man's face, that we might look on Him always. He will never fail you, but will hear you and help you in your time of need. Yet there is one who lives in darkness, and his home is the house of falsehood, and his kingdom the realm of hell! Love the truth and turn your mind away from his lies, and don't waver between his ways and the ways of God. My son, nothing comes easy. If you are to realize your dreams, you must be willing to work hard and serve others.

With those words ringing in his head, right then and there, the long-legged boy decided that he would step up and take responsibility for the curly-haired girl and the baby she was carrying. Suddenly, his heart turned on like a bright light. But was it too late?

Urgently, he bounded with his long legs up the stairs and into the building, his heart pounding in his chest. When he entered, he found the curly-haired girl getting her money back from the receptionist.

Responsibility: Being accountable or answerable, as for a trust.

"You didn't do it, did you?" he cried. "Come on! Let's get out of here!"

As the two of them climbed back into the van and got ready to drive away from that place of death, the long-legged boy turned to the curly-haired girl and asked, "Will you marry me?" With a big smile, she said yes. And they embarked on a whole new chapter of their life as soon-to-be husband and wife that was to include the son she was carrying and later, a daughter.

Words Remembered

The parting words given to the long-legged boy and curly-haired girl by those who cared and wanted the best for them were not heard when they were first spoken. But they came to mind at an important moment and changed everything. Even though those two were not good listeners and made plenty of mistakes along the way, God found them and brought them to himself.

In the words of the long-legged boy's mother, *"God wore a man's face, that we might look on Him always."* His mother's words were true—Jesus, though he is God, wears the face of a man so that we may look to him forever as our example and our friend. There is no more beautiful, loving, or compassionate face than his.

When the long-legged boy finally accepted responsibility for his actions, he left behind his warrior daydreams and started his journey as a true spiritual warrior in the Great Battle under the banner of the Victorious Warrior. He saw the one who lies in darkness, whose home is the house of falsehood, for what he is: a liar and a destroyer.

In the words of the curly-haired girl's neighbor, *"There is One who watches over you, and in your darkest hour of need, He will find you, make you His own, and give you a home where you belong."* Her neighbor's words were true—God had watched over the curly-haired girl and found her in her darkest hour. He gave her a home in his kingdom and a feeling of belonging that she could not find anywhere else. She understood that she must give herself to Jesus and resist the evil one who lives in shadows—the one who had already done so much damage in her life. She became a spiritual warrior in the Great Battle alongside the long-legged boy.

Grace beyond Measure

The long-legged boy and curly-haired girl made every mistake imaginable, yet it was God's plan all along to make a place for them in his kingdom. How on earth could this be? How undeserved! How unlikely! They both came to recognize God's presence in their lives as a loving, guiding Creator who sent his Son so that they could be free from their sin—even their awful sin of abortion. They accepted the forgiveness of Jesus with all their hearts and on their knees. In deepest gratitude they praised God for bringing them from darkness into the light of a new life.

Many marriages with the challenges faced by the long-legged boy and the curly-haired girl fall apart. But with Jesus in the middle of their marriage, they overcame. They discovered their identity in the love God extended to them.

> Those words of wisdom spoken to our two drifters then quickly forgotten by them—and finally remembered and cherished—those words are for you also.

Now they are warriors in the army of the Victorious Warrior, and they fight in the spiritual battle for good and against evil. They aim toward the good, and they have taken on Jesus's commission and commandment to love others and tell the world about the new life to be found with Jesus.

Those words of wisdom spoken to our two drifters then quickly forgotten by them—and finally remembered and cherished—those words are for you also. God became man so that you might know him. He lived as a man and died to take the punishment for your sin. He sees you in your darkest hour. His death frees you and gives you eternal life in your true home, the place where you belong—with him in his kingdom. And if, like the long-legged boy and curly-haired girl, you have made every mistake imaginable, you are not beyond God's reach. Undeserved and unlikely as it may be, he has a place for you in his kingdom. This is the good news.

As you may have already figured out, the long-legged boy and curly-haired girl are your authors. We've embellished some of the details of our story, but the main facts are exactly as you have read them. Our greatest hope is that our mistakes will be used by God to help you live your best life, far away from the pitfalls of life apart from God. The sooner you set yourself on a path alongside the Victorious Warrior, Jesus, the sooner you will find your identity as that extraordinary pearl for which the merchant was willing to give everything he had.

It's who you are.

Because of who he is.

And who you are is priceless.

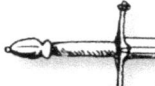

> *Then I heard a loud voice shouting across the heavens, "It has come at last—salvation and power and the Kingdom of our God, and the authority of his Christ. For the accuser of our brothers and sisters has been thrown down to earth—the one who accuses them before our God day and night. And they have defeated him by the blood of the Lamb and by their testimony. And they did not love their lives so much that they were afraid to die."* (**Revelation 12:10-11**)[1]

The evil one is defeated. He was defeated by the blood shed by the Lamb of God, Jesus Christ. And your testimony is part of Jesus's victory story. Yes, you have a testimony! The Victorious Warrior is in your midst, and he is rejoicing over you with joy. Jesus is your Victorious Warrior, fighting for you and fighting alongside you. In him, you have the victory!

---

1. New Living Translation.

Some questions for you:

1. What do you imagine the people praying outside the office were saying to God?

2. What terrible life mistakes does God refuse to forgive?

3. Did you know all along as you were reading this book that the long-legged boy and curly-haired were your authors telling their own story?

Notes:

17 • Onward, Christian Soldiers

We began this book together by entering into a thought experiment. You imagined yourself as a valiant warrior, decked out in shining armor and with a flashing blade by your side. You imagined you were on a special mission with a highly trained team, under orders from the king himself, chosen because you had proven yourself well trained, loyal, and a person of character. With the help of this king and with your special training, you imagined that you were able to complete your mission and be victorious.

If you have decided to stand with the Victorious Warrior, Jesus, this thought experiment is now reality. You are developing the warrior's mindset. You are dressed in the spiritual armor of God. By your side is your sword, which is God's word that we find in the Bible. And truly, you are on a special God-given mission with a team of warriors who all follow Jesus. You are under orders from God himself. He considers you trustworthy because of your dedication to becoming a spiritual warrior. With his help and with your warrior's mindset, you are able to complete his mission and be victorious.

But what is God's mission for you? Your mission and purpose are to believe in Jesus, to follow his teachings and learn more about him, and to tell other people of his goodness so that they, too, can be part of the kingdom of God.

The good news, or Gospel, of Jesus is what gives you meaning and purpose in this life and a forward-looking hope of heaven after you die.

By now you see that the hero of this book is the Victorious Warrior, Jesus. The life of the spiritual warrior can be very challenging, but you have his daily partnership, support, and help through prayer, Bible reading, and fellowship with other Christians. Aiming toward the good and following your code with a warrior's mindset will take you out of your comfort zone and stretch you in ways you never thought you could be stretched. By rising to the challenge to do things you didn't think you could do—things ordinary people don't attempt—you grow. Don't be afraid to do things that are hard.

Spiritual warriors are no ordinary people. They aim toward the good and practice loving truth, pursuing excellence, and serving others. They are the boss of their desires. They are aware that they are in a spiritual battle against a very real enemy, and they rely on Jesus to strengthen them and assure them of the victory. These warriors are made extraordinary by his power. They belong to an army that is a multitude stretching around the globe and including all races and nationalities, without boundaries—an army that stretches across the ages from millennia past to the present and beyond into the future. All who believe and follow Jesus, the Victorious Warrior, are part of his army.

> Jesus is your example, your help, your salvation, your rescuer when you fail, and your number-one fan.

Jesus will grow you day by day more and more into his likeness if you allow him. He is your example, your help, your salvation, your rescuer when you fail, and your number-one fan. Jesus wants more than anything for you to place your trust in him and let him shape you into the best version of yourself that you can be. "Victory is found not just at the end of the road. It is in every humble step we take every day to reach the end of the road."[1]

---

1. Gabriel Porras, "The Power of Myths," *Radiant Whispers*, RadiantWhispers.com.

A New Chapter

Because you have taken this step and claimed your place in the army of God, aiming toward the good, you need to be aware that you now have what Jesus calls a Great Commission. This is your new assignment: to invite others to learn of Jesus and join you in the kingdom of God. Here is how Jesus says it:

> *Go and make followers of all people in the world.... Teach them to obey everything that I have told you to do.* (Matthew 28:19-20)

You stand alongside some of the most extraordinary warriors in history who have dedicated themselves to live for Jesus and spread the word about his love. You are part of a glorious legacy of service in that Great Battle. You stand on the shoulders of such inspiring warriors as Matthew, Mark, Luke, and John, the apostle Paul, Saint Francis of Assisi, Joan of Arc, William Tyndale, George Washington, William Wilberforce, Sojourner Truth, David Livingston, and Blessed Mother Teresa, among countless others—most of whose names are remembered only by God.

Here is a hymn written over one hundred and fifty years ago that speaks of the spiritual warrior who goes into battle against the evil one with "the cross of Jesus going on before!" Celebrate your victory under the banner of Jesus as *hell's foundations quiver at your shout of praise!*

Onward, Christian Soldiers

Onward, Christian soldiers, marching as to war,
With the cross of Jesus going on before!
Christ, the royal Master, leads against the foe;
Forward into battle, see his banner go!

Onward, Christian soldiers, marching as to war,
With the cross of Jesus going on before!

At the sign of triumph Satan's host doth flee;
On, then, Christian soldiers, on to victory!
Hell's foundations quiver at the shout of praise;
Brothers, lift your voices, loud your anthems raise!

Like a mighty army moves the church of God;
Brothers, we are treading where the saints have trod;
We are not divided; all one body we,
One in hope and doctrine, one in charity.

Onward, then, ye people, join our happy throng,
Blend with ours your voices in the triumph song;
Glory, laud, and honor, unto Christ the King;
This thro' countless ages men and angels sing.[2]

2. Sabine Baring-Gould, text; Arthur S. Sullivan, music, "Onward Christian Soldiers," 1864.

Some questions for you:

1. How has becoming a spiritual warrior stretched you and challenged you?

2. How has the life of Jesus been an example to you? How has Jesus been a friend to you?

3. Can you think of someone you know who may be interested in hearing the good news about Jesus?

Notes:

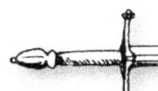

May the Lord bless you and keep you. May the Lord smile down on you and show you his kindness. May the Lord answer your prayers and give you peace. (**Numbers 6:24-26**)

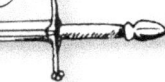

Art Credits

We offer our tribute of thanksgiving to Chrétien de Troyes's work, *Perceval*, which inspired our story, particularly the words of wisdom offered to our two heroes.

Most of the drawings in this book were drawn from great examples of art found in the public domain, thanks to Wikimedia Commons {{Public Domain}}:

Yoshitoshi Taiso, "Ronin"

Philippe Jacques de Loutherbourg, "Vision of the White Horse"

Hokusai, "Archers"

"Turning Bear, Sioux Warrior"

Charles William Meredith van de Velde, "Le Pays d'Israel"

Hans Burgkmair, "The Triumph of Maximilian I"

Adolf Rosenberg, Eduard Heck, "Geschichte des Kostüms"

Renata, "Chessboard in Blackwork Embroidery, Using Holbein Stitch"

Tomasz Sienicki, "Nautical Compass"

Magnetic compasses, 1940

Joan Blaeu, "Map of Yugorsky Strait," 1659

Sarah Brewer Bonebright, "Reminiscences of Newcastle, Iowa"

Josef Manes, "St. George"

Theodore de Boy, "Nova Zembla and the Northeast Passage"

Giovanni Battista Cavallini, "Atlas Nautiche de la Mer Méditerranée"

David Daniel Davis, "The Principles and Practices of Obstetric Medicine"

Thaler, "Magyar: Festetics-palota"

Antonio del Ceraiolo, "St. Lawrence"

Alain Manesson Mallet, "View of Yerevan, Description de L'Universe" (1685) and "Plan de l'église du Saint Sépulchre et du Mont-Calvaire à Jérusalem" (1683)

Albrecht Dürer, "St. Hubertus, auch Eustachius genannt"

Bookman Ornaments

Gertrud Caspari, "Kinderhumor Storch"

Gordon Ross, "Matrimonial Primer"

Nederlands: Afbeelding van tien heraldische kronen, bekroningen van een wapen.

Book Cover for Leon Gautier's "La Chevalerie (Chivalry)"

"A Zulu Warrior," from Joseph Forsyth Ingram's *The Lands of Gold, Diamonds and Ivory*

We thank the following Pixabay artists for their pattern and other miscellaneous art:

David Zydd, Yousz, Yoytu, Merio, Aquamarine_song, GDJ, bjcox86, Arsty-Bee, Ginger Tea, Pexels, GDJ, Geralt, Yayangart, Kan-art, Clker-Free-Vector-Images, Graphicnet

Author Resources

You can find additional resources and lesson ideas for each chapter at: VictoriousWarrior.org.

For book orders, email info@RaeLochPublishing.com.

Authors Jerry and Michelle Shelfer run a nonprofit called Prepare a Room Ministries, which exists to offer the healing work of the cross to those hurt by abortion and the culture of death. This ministry can be found at:

PrepareaRoom.com

TheFoundlings.net

@PrepareaRoom

PREPARE A ROOM:

A Path to Peace and Healing for Those Hurt by Abortion

by Michelle Shelfer

A CULTURE OF DENIAL about the traumatic effects of abortion has left many women and men trapped in regret, shame, and self-condemnation about their experience. Michelle Shelfer offers a ten-step path to peace and healing that addresses the damage done to identity and relationships and offers real-life tools to restore what has been broken. Embark on a journey that honors your unique story and opens the door to restoration through discovery of the greatest love.

www.ingramcontent.com/pod-product-compliance
Lightning Source LLC
Chambersburg PA
CBHW041513120626
46551CB00018B/2408